SOUTHERN OREGON WILDERNESS AREAS

by
Donna Ikenberry Aitkenhead

Photographs by Donna & Roger
Aitkenhead

The Touchstone Press
P.O. Box 81
Beaverton, Oregon 97075

Cover photos: *Mt. Thielsen*
Blossom Creek
Red Lake

I.S.B.N. No. 0-911518-78-9
Copyright© 1988
by Donna Ikenberry Aitkenhead & Roger Aitkenhead
Maps Courtesy U.S. Geological Survey

For
Beverly Bruer Ikenberry,
my Mom

Dairy Creek with Gearhart Mountain in background

contents

Castle Rock in the Rogue–Umpqua Divide Wilderness

SOUTHERN OREGON WILDERNESS AREAS

INTRODUCTION

(Author's note: During the summer of 1987 severe fires raged through much of southern Oregon and into some of the Wilderness Areas described in this guide. It is therefore possible that some signs and/or buildings described in the text may be missing. It would be wise to check with the Forest Service officials regarding the particular Wilderness you choose to enter to see what, if any, portions of it were damaged by the fire.)

Wilderness. To some folks the word means a trip to the local city park, ice chests full, baseball equipment tucked away in the trunks of their cars. To others wilderness is a unique experience whereby one hikes through the woods, enjoying the peace and solitude of an uncrowded land, touching a delicate wildflower, keeping ever alert while watching for signs of birds, mammals, and other denizens of the forest. Regardless of each individual interpretation of "what is wilderness?", as defined by this book it is subject to those areas designated by Congress as a result of the Wilderness Act of 1964.

In 1956 the first wilderness bill was introduced in Congress by Hubert Humphrey, then the Democratic senator from Minnesota. Also supporting Humphrey was John P. Saylor, a Republican House Member from Pennsylvania, and nine co-sponsors. In 1964, after nearly twenty hearings, the bill was finally passed. According to the law, wilderness "shall be administered for the use and enjoyment of the American people in such a manner as will leave them unimpaired for future use and enjoyment as wilderness, and so as to provide for the protection of these areas (and) the preservation of their wilderness character."

Currently there are thirty-six Wilderness areas in Oregon, ten of which are located in the southern portion of the state and listed in this book. To date, over two million acres have been designated Wilderness in the Beaver state with 519,988 of those acres found in southern Oregon and the vast majority managed by the National Forest Service.

Throughout the United States, the National Wilderness Preservation System consists of thirty-two million acres. Although solitude can be found in the majority, some areas are attractive to too many people, with overcrowding a growing problem. And the problem is expected to increase in severity. In his book, *Battle for the Wilderness*, Michael Frome states that as of 1974 the government was forecasting a wilderness use increase of one thousand percent by the year 2000.

In 1986, over 12 million visitor days (each day being one 12-hour period) were recorded for the wilderness, a substantial increase from the 4.5 million persons who visited a wilderness area in 1965. In Oregon alone, 1.6 million visitor days were recorded for the wilderness in 1986 versus just over one-half million in 1982.

The need to preserve and protect areas such as these are far greater than one might imagine. In a crowded world filled with black-topped roads and cemented cities, it is comforting to know that small pockets of land have been set aside to enjoy as God once intended. Can you really blame the people who are anxious to escape from the city and visit a land of pristine beauty once in a while? Of course not! But something must be done to protect the human race from loving the land to death.

There are many do's and do not's in relation to managing a wilderness. Primitive methods of travel are allowed. You may backpack, day hike, ride a horse, or pack in with your favorite animal such as: a horse, mule, llama, or even a backpacking dog. But, motorcycles, mountain bikes, and other mechanical or motorized methods of travel are not allowed.

Some wilderness visitors do not agree with the policy, but mining and cattle grazing are allowed in some areas. As long as a mining claim is valid, mining is allowed, but with rules and regulations that must be adhered to. Also, cattle grazing is allowed if cattle were grazing on the land prior to the area becoming a designated wilderness. Again, certain rules apply.

But basically the wilderness is a place, "where man is a visitor who does not remain." To permit others the same wonderful experience that you might find in the wilderness please remember the following:

1. "Take only pictures, leave only footprints" are six words that everyone should remember. It is against the law to pick flowers or to remove Indian artifacts. If you want to remember a special moment, a precious flower, etc., take photographs. And leave footprints only on the trails. Do not make trails wider by skirting around the drier edges of a muddy trail. Plow right through. Don't take short-cuts.

2. All backpackers should carry a portable camp stove. Everyone loves a nice warm campfire, but if wood is scarce please use a stove. If you do build a fire use existing fire rings and be sure your campfire is dead out when you leave.
3. If everyone would pack out what they pack in wouldn't the world be a cleaner place to live? Please pack out all of your garbage. Do not bury garbage as wild animals will dig it up. If you burn your garbage remember foil and cans don't burn. Carry them out.
4. Those packing into the wilderness will find a 10 or 12 person/animal group limit consisting of, for example 6 people, 6 pack animals, or 8 people, 4 pack animals. Stock owners should note that feed should be carried into the wilderness. Also, animals should be picketed at least 200 feet from any water source. And hikers should remain on the down side of the trail when horseback riders or packers meet on the trail.
5. Fishing and hunting permits are required.
6. Although dogs are allowed in all ten southern Oregon wilderness areas many object to them being there. But we disagree. A restrained, well-mannered, quiet dog should be no problem at all. Predators at heart, dogs will seize every opportunity to chase the birds and animals of the forest. Please restrain your pet at all times to prevent mishaps.
7. Do not feed the wildlife. Leftover food may carry bacteria that is harmful to wildlife and animals can become dependent on humans for food.
8. Try to camp more than 100 feet from water and avoid camping in meadows, on top of flowers, and in wet places.
9. Dispose of human waste properly. Using the cat method, dig a hole 6 to 8 inches deep, setting the top soil aside. After eliminating waste, cover up the hole, place soil back on top, and if possible cover with a rock.
10. Wash your body, clothes, and dishes away from streams, springs, and lakes. Do not use any soap, including biodegradeable, while standing in the water source. Move 100 feet away and wash there. And bury your toothpaste.

One special warning about drinking the water you will find rushing in rivers, cascading down rocky creeks, trickling down streams, and seeping from natural springs. The water may contain organisms that cause giardiasis, also known as backpackers' diarrhea. Persons drinking from these water sources should boil the water for three to five minutes before drinking or using in food preparation. Water purifiers and commercial water purification chemicals are also available, but are not always effective in killing the organisms.

The above suggestions are not intended to prevent someone from enjoying their stay, but rather to insure a good time for our generation and next and the next and all those who follow. May God bless you and yours while you are visiting the wilderness, whether it be for one hour, one day, one week, or a month or more.

SPECIAL NOTE: The Forest Service has informed me that some of the signs mentioned in this guidebook may be removed in the future due to a move to eliminate man-made objects in the wilderness.

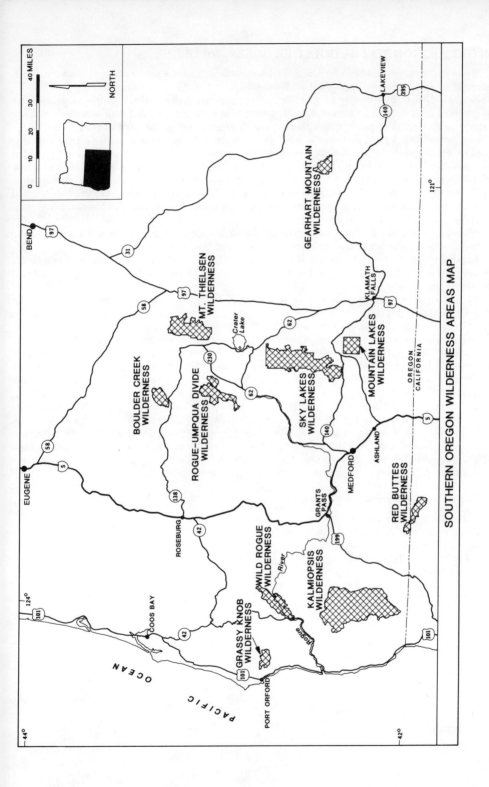

SOUTHERN OREGON WILDERNESS AREAS MAP

INTRODUCTION TO THE BOULDER CREEK WILDERNESS

Steep and rugged, the Boulder Creek Wilderness is rich in old growth forest, numerous rock monoliths, small streams, and plant and animal life.

Boulder Creek, a tributary of the North Umpqua River, flows through the middle of the Wilderness, its waters an important spawning stream for anadromous fish. Small waterfalls, rushing rapids, and tiny, quiet pools, combine to make Boulder Creek a nice spot to visit.

Designated Wilderness on June 26, 1984, Boulder Creek Wilderness is located on the west side of the Cascade Mountains, 50 miles east of Roseburg, Oregon. The 19,100 acre area is located in and managed by the Umpqua National Forest. The Wilderness ranges in elevation from a low of 1,600 feet near the southern boundary to a high of 5,600 feet near the northern boundary.

There are some interesting geologic areas to visit in the southern portion. At Pine Bench you'll find a 140 acre stand of old growth ponderosa pine, a rarity for an area this far north and west of the summit of the Cascades.

Also of interest is the Umpqua rocks geological area, comprised of spires of basalt and interesting cliffs, located partially within the southern portion of the Wilderness.

For those who would like to fish in Boulder Creek please note that state regulations require fly fishing only. There are rainbow and cutthroat trout in the creek, but they are usually small and hardly worth keeping.

There are plenty of wildflowers for everyone to enjoy during the spring and early summer months. See, smell and touch these beautiful wonders of nature, but please don't pick them. Give others the chance to enjoy the beauty of each delicate wildflower.

Wildlife lovers will be interested in knowing there are black bear and mountain lions roaming the area. Of course, they are rarely encountered, but there is always a thrill in just knowing they are there. The Forest Service claims they have not experienced problems with either animal. In addition to bear and mountain lion, you may also find deer, elk, spotted owl and many other species which inhabit the Boulder Creek Wilderness.

An unwelcome critter—the mosquito—appears in the spring after snow melt. There are quite a few of the pests at this time of the year, but there are less mosquitoes here than at higher elevations.

Portions of the Wilderness are generally accessible year-round. Those areas below 2,500 feet are usually free of snow, but the higher elevations receive an average of four to five feet of snow. The area is usually snowfree from mid-June to early November. Spring and fall are the best times to visit the Wilderness as temperatures can be quite hot in the summer.

For further information contact:

Umpqua National Forest
Diamond Lake Ranger District
HC 60 Box 101
Idleyld Park, OR 97447
(503) 498-2531

Boulder Creek

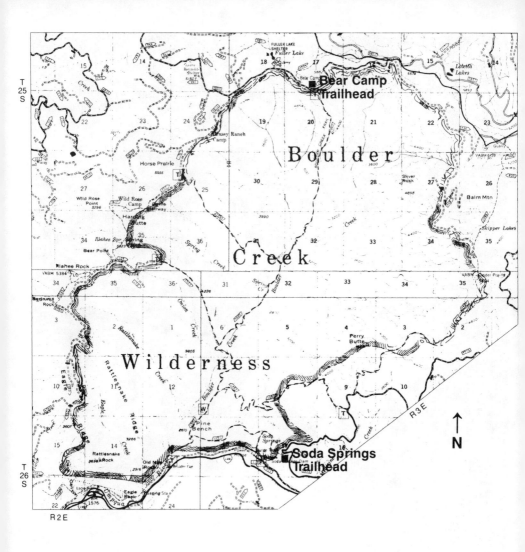

SOUTHERN OREGON WILDERNESS AREAS

1 BOULDER CREEK TRAIL

Distance: 10.3 miles
Elevation gain: 830 feet; loss: 4,290 feet
High point: 5,300 feet
Usually open: Mid-June through early
November
Topographic map: Rogue-Umpqua Divide,
Boulder Creek and
Mt. Thielsen Wilder-
nesses Map
Obtain map from: Umpqua National Forest

There are several trails leading into the Boulder Creek Wilderness with the Boulder Creek Trail stretching from the southern end of the Wilderness to the northern end. In addition, the maintained trail is sometimes located parallel to the creek, sometimes not. Backpackers will travel through old growth forest while hiking the Boulder Creek Trail.

Hikers may want to leave a vehicle at the Soda Springs Trailhead and have someone shuttle them up to the Bear Camp Trailhead at the north end of the Wilderness. (See following guide for instructions.)

The Soda Springs Trailhead is located a couple of miles west of Tokatee off Oregon Hwy. 138. At the "Soda Spring Reservoir" sign head north and immediately make a left on the dirt road. Follow this road past the dam, across the bridge, and park at the Soda Springs Trailhead, 1.3 miles from Oregon Hwy. 138. The trail begins at a small bridge located under the large water pipe.

To reach the Bear Camp Trailhead drive to the junction of Oregon Hwy. 138 and FS Road No. 38 at Steamboat. Head northeast on FS Road No. 38 reaching FS Road No. 3817 in 11.0 miles. Turn right on No. 3817 and continue on this for 3.0 miles to FS Road No. 3850. Head down FS Road No. 3850 for 8.0 miles. (FS Road No. 3850 turns into FS No. 3810 at this point.) Continue down FS Road No. 3810 for 1.5 miles. Continue to broken-down sign pointing to Boulder Creek Wilderness.

Begin descending Boulder Creek Trail No. 1552, entering the Wilderness by switchback in a few hundred yards. Continue the switchbacks to 0.6 mile. Now the trail will gradually descend and occasionally climb as you make your way to Boulder Creek. At 2.6 miles descend a series of steep switchbacks. Reach Boulder Creek at 3.3 miles. There is a campsite at this spot.

Continue down the trail to the point where Boulder Creek and an unnamed creek meet. Cross Boulder Creek and reunite with the trail as it runs along the east side of Boulder Creek. Hike up the hill, then down to a log which crosses in front of the trail. Cross the creek at this point, then head downstream for 50 feet, continuing along the west side of the creek.

At 3.5 miles the creek cascades over some pretty rocks. Continue a few hundred feet farther to find another campsite, although it isn't quite as nice as the first one. There are two trails at this point. Boulder Creek Trail heads to the right and continues along the right side of the fire pit. The trail to the left runs down to the creek and stops.

Continue to 3.8 miles and the confluence of Boulder Creek and an unnamed creek. Cross Boulder Creek, then hike along the unnamed creek until the trail ends a short distance ahead. Cross the creek and follow the trail as it heads back near the east side of Boulder Creek.

At 4.2 miles cross back to the west side of Boulder Creek. A fine camp is on the top of this hill. Continue through the camp down the trail to Spring Creek. Cross Spring Creek where it meets Boulder Creek and continue down on the west side of Boulder Creek. Be careful not to take some of the side trails leading to the creek!

At 5.0 miles head away and uphill from the creek. At 5.5 miles the trail heads downhill reaching Spring Mountain Trail at 5.9 miles. Stay straight and continue to the switchbacks at 6.1 miles. Hike a few switchbacks before descending to the junction of Onion Creek and Boulder Creek at 6.3 miles. Cross Boulder Creek. There's a nice camp on this shore though it is too close to the creek—approximately 30 feet. Please note that this is your last chance to obtain water at Boulder Creek.

As you leave the creek, climb steeply then descend and climb again to 7.2 miles and the junction of Perry Butte Trail. Keep straight, continuing on to 7.6 miles. You'll see a trail heading north off the Boulder Creek Trail at this point. Take the north trail a few hundred yards to a large rock outcropping. There is a view of the valley below from this point although trees block much of the view.

Return to the Boulder Creek Trail. After a hundred yards or so you'll see some good spots for camping if you've brought plenty of water. There is a spring near the overlook, but the Forest Service reports that the spring is typically dry early in the season and that there is a problem with the parasite, giardiasis.

Notice the large stand of Ponderosa pine trees in this area known as Pine Bench. Pine Bench consists of a 140 acre stand of Ponderosa pine believed to be the largest such stand this far north and west of the summit of the Cascade Mountains.

At 8.3 miles reach the junction of the Boulder Creek Trail and the Bradley Trail. Turn left onto the Bradley Trail No. 1491 and hike the level trail to the switchbacks which moderately descend to the Soda Stub Trail junction at 9.8 miles. Take the Soda Stub Trail to the right and gradually descend to the trailhead at 10.3 miles.

Mule Deer

SOUTHERN OREGON WILDERNESS AREAS

Blazed tree near trail

INTRODUCTION TO THE GEARHART MOUNTAIN WILDERNESS

Vertical walls of rock, delicate meadows, wildlife and wildflowers, a sapphire blue lake, and breathtaking views make Gearhart Mountain Wilderness a real treat for those traveling to this part of Oregon.

The Gearhart Mountain Wilderness is located deep in the Fremont National Forest of south-central Oregon, 12 airline miles from Bly. Bly is the nearest town to the Wilderness, providing supplies such as gasoline, food, and other essentials.

The Wilderness was first established on November 11, 1943 by the Forest Service. Named Gearhart Wild Area, and totalling 18,709 acres, it was noted for its high elevation, scenic overlooks, rock formations, and was also one of the few remaining roadless areas in this part of Oregon.

Twenty one years later, in 1964, Congress designated all National Forest Wild areas as Wilderness areas. And with the passage of the Wilderness Act, the Gearhart Wild Area was renamed the Gearhart Mountain Wilderness.

Today, it consists of 22,809 acres due to an increase of 4,100 acres by the Oregon Wilderness Act of 1984. At the present time there are no plans to increase the size of this Wilderness.

Gearhart Mountain, rising 8,354 feet above sea level, the most prominent feature, was formed by volcanic flows and plugs of porphyritic lava. Scientists believe that once this mountain was a massive dome standing at least 10,000 feet high. As the land and climate cooled, ice formed. Enormous snowfields and glaciers blanketed the dome for thousands of years. Once again the land warmed, melting the ice, and carving the U-shaped valleys we see today.

There are three trails leading into the Wilderness, all with special features of their own. From the south entrance, at Corral Creek, you'll hike among giant rock formations known as the Palisades. From there the trail leads into the forest where you'll get a chance to peek out from among the trees and see a variety of distant sights including Mt. Shasta, an amazing one hundred miles away.

From the north entrance the trail travels through open pine stands, small meadows, and thick stands of fir and lodgepole pine. This brand-new trail leads to Blue Lake, the only lake within the Gearhart Mountain Wilderness. Surrounded by pines and firs, the clear and always cold waters of this lake are situated in a glacially formed depression.

From the west side of the Wilderness you'll climb the Demming Creek Trail which follows Demming Creek for part of the way, rejoining the original Boulder Creek Trail just below Boulder Springs.

Regardless of where you begin, all trails lead to Gearhart Mountain. As you approach the mountain notice that it appears to be split in two, both halves standing side-by-side. The northern-most half is called "The Notch" and breaks off from the main peak for more than 300 feet.

When viewing Gearhart Mountain from the east, the sheer rock cliffs make a summit climb without the use of technical mountaineering equipment seem all but impossible. Although there isn't a trail leading to the top, the summit can be easily reached by climbing the dominant south ridge. From Gearhart's highest point you'll see (on a clear day) Steens Mountain to the east, Blue Lake to the northeast, and towards the west you'll gaze at a variety of Cascade Peaks extending from Mt. Lassen in California to the Three Sisters in Oregon.

Observing plant life and animals are always an added plus when hiking in the wilderness and the Gearhart Mountain Wilderness is no exception. During spring and early summer, wildflowers splash their bright colors against the lush green meadows, like a child with his first set of finger paints. And if you're one of the lucky ones you may catch a glimpse of a trophy buck walking silently through the woods, or hear a bull elk bugling during the crisp days of autumn. Maybe you'll see a mountain lion, a bear, a bobcat, or a coyote. Birdwatchers might see a variety of warblers, woodpeckers, jays, or owls and perhaps a blue grouse, or two or three.

Gearhart is a small area with limited trails. The Forest Service recommends that the trails into it be used by small groups. Stock animals are allowed into the Wilderness although forage is not readily available except in the moist meadows where the plant community is fragile.

Trails are maintained each summer by Forest Service employees or volunteers. If you plan to hike early in the season be prepared to cross over or hike around fallen trees and be sure to bring plenty of bug repellent to ward off pesky mosquitoes.

Cattle grazing in the area will annoy some people. Cattle tend to concentrate in the fragile meadows where water and foraging material is available and spend little time in the dense forest where the grazing is poor. As a result, loss of vegetation due to heavy browsing on riparian shrubs is evident in some areas. Humans have created some eyesores as well. Remember, "leave only footprints, take only memories."

You can gather memories anytime of the year at the Gearhart Mountain Wilderness. The best times for backpacking are after the snow melts off the trails sometime during late June or July. Trails usually stay snow free until late October or early November.

Once the snow begins to fall you can explore the upper elevations of the Wilderness using cross-country skis or snowshoes. With the gentle terrain found at Gearhart, the avalanche danger is low. Access is the biggest problem when trying to ski or snowshoe at Gearhart, as the roads are usually blocked by snow. A call to the Bly Ranger District will provide a current road report.

When visiting the Wilderness in winter be prepared for very cold temperatures and numerous snow storms. This means highs around freezing or colder, and lows down to perhaps minus 40 degrees. During the summer you can expect highs near 80 and lows in the 30's. Also, you can expect a sudden afternoon or evening thunderstorm anytime.

The Gearhart Mountain Wilderness is a land of extreme temperatures, gentle streams, tall pines, and spectacular viewpoints.

For more information contact the following:

Fremont National Forest
Forest Supervisor's Office
P.O. Box 551   or
Lakeview, OR 97630
(503) 947-2151

Fremont National Forest
Bly Ranger District
Bly, OR 97622
(503) 353-2427

Blue Lake

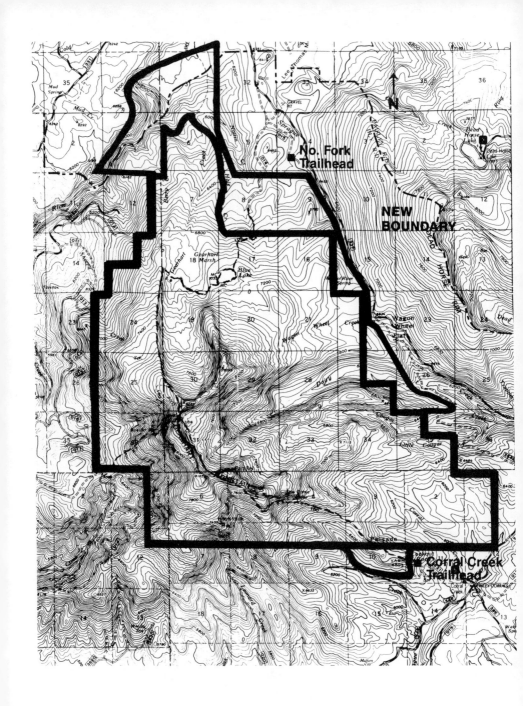

2   CORRAL CREEK TRAILHEAD to the NOTCH

Distance: 6.2 miles
Elevation gain: 1,920 feet; loss: 120 feet
High point: 8,040 feet
Usually open: Mid-June through late
October or November
Topographic map: The Gearhart Mountain
Wilderness Map
Obtain map from: Fremont National Forest

Corral Creek is one of three access points leading into the Gearhart Mountain Wilderness. With this trailhead as a starting point, hikers will pass through the unusual rock formations known as the Palisades and lush Dairy Creek Meadow while enroute to the Notch.

To reach the trailhead at Corral Creek take Oregon Hwy. 140 to FS Road No. 348, one mile east of Bly. A sign, "Gearhart Wilderness Area— 17 miles" leads the way. Head north on FS Road No. 348 for 0.4 mile. At this point there is a large water tank on your left. Turn to the right and follow FS Road No. 348 to Corral Creek Rd. and follow this one-way dirt road 1.3 miles to the trailhead, which is located at the northwest end of the parking area.

It's an easy hike on Gearhart Trail No. 100 to the Wilderness boundary at 0.6 mile. Continue a short distance farther for a hike through the Palisades. Massive porphyritic lava flows created this unique group of rock formations. Hikers will enjoy the easy hike through this unusual area where Ponderosa pine stand scattered throughout the rocky terrain and yellow clumps of wildflowers brighten up the hard surface.

After passing through the Palisades, the trail drops down into the trees then gradually climbs through tall pines, lush ferns, and in the summer you'll find a wide variety of wildflowers. At 1.8 miles begin to climb moderately. At 2.4 miles (just before the trail heads east toward The Dome) you'll hear the refreshing sound of running water. This is the first fresh water since starting out. (Take the path to the left for water and a great spot for a picnic.)

Continue on the Gearhart Trail, climbing moderately. As you approach the Dome notice the cliffs of this 7,380 foot mountain. Like a great fortress, they stretch westward for three-fourths of a mile and rise 300 to 400 feet above the embracing terrain.

Continue past the Dome. As you round a lazy horseshoe turn at 3.3 miles be sure to look for Mt. Shasta off in the distance towards the southwest. Unbelievable, Mt. Shasta is over 100 miles away. Just before reaching a saddle at 4.4 miles you'll come to a sign claiming "6 miles to Lookout Rock, 6 miles to Blue Lake." The Forest Service has informed me that the trail has changed a bit since that sign was first erected so it's now partially incorrect. You've traveled 4.4 miles from Lookout Rock, and you have a 6 mile hike to Blue Lake.

Continue to the saddle for a spectacular view looking both north and south. If you've carried water up to this point and want to make camp you're in luck. There are a couple of nice camping areas at this 7,920 foot site.

When leaving the saddle head north down a small incline then follow the trail to the west across the shale slope. Follow the trail north again through the forest. At 4.6 miles you'll reach a small creek. Cross here and continue along the easy trail. At 4.9 miles you'll reach Dairy Creek, which flows year-round, so fill up on water if necessary. It's also the last dependable source of water until you reach Blue Lake.

This wide open meadow is especially beautiful in early summer when wildflowers abound. An excellent view of the steep rock walls of Gearhart Mountain provide a real treat, too. Cross the creek at the Forest Service sign, "Head Dairy Creek," and continue across the meadow and back into the forest. This section of trail is especially inviting for it provides many views of Gearhart Mountain and the trail is relatively flat.

At 5.7 miles the trail turns to the right and heads east and away from Gearhart. At 5.8 miles the trail bends in a U-turn and heads back towards Gearhart. Reach the highest point along the Gearhart Trail, 8,040 feet, at 6.2 miles. Also, please note, there is a close-up view of the Notch from this point.

(If you'd like to continue your hike to the northern boundary of the Gearhart Wilderness you'll find #3 NORTH FORK TRAILHEAD TO THE NOTCH most helpful.)

Rocky Mountain bull elk

SOUTHERN OREGON WILDERNESS AREAS

Hiking through Palisade Rocks

3 NORTH FORK TRAILHEAD to the NOTCH

Distance: 7.2 miles
Elevation gain: 1,680 feet; loss: 0 feet
High point: 8,040 feet
Usually open: Mid-June or mid-July through late October
Topographic map: The Gearhart Mountain Wilderness Map
Obtain map from: Fremont National Forest

Anglers will enjoy this trip because the trail passes alongside beautiful Blue Lake. And wildlife enthusiasts will find it is possible to see Rocky Mountain elk in the Gearhart Marsh. All this, in addition to a grand view of the Gearhart Mountain Wilderness from a point near the Notch.

To reach the North Fork Trailhead drive Oregon Hwy. 140 to FS Road No. 348, one mile east of Bly. A sign, "Gearhart Wilderness Area–17 miles" leads the way. Head north on FS Road No. 348 for 0.4 mile. At this point there is a large water tank on your left. Turn to the right and follow FS Road No. 348 to FS Road No. 337 at 19.3 miles. Turn left on FS Road No. 337 and head northwest along the east side of the Gearhart Wilderness for about 9.0 miles. Turn left on FS Road No. 015 and remain on this road until you reach the North Fork Trailhead at 1.5 miles.

This trailhead, and the first section of trail you'll begin hiking on, was built during the late summer of 1986, a couple of months after we visited the area via the Blue Lake Trailhead located off FS Road No. 014. The Forest Service has informed me that the new alignment is a much more interesting trail and more scenic, too.

The trail winds through open pine stands and thick stands of fir and lodgepole pine, sometimes passing through small meadows. Water can be found at two springs during part of the year, but the springs do not flow year-round. The trail climbs gently with a couple of short grades to Blue Lake at 3.1 miles.

Blue Lake is stocked with trout by the Oregon Department of Fish and Wildlife, which each year dumps about 3,000 fingerling rainbow trout into the lake via helicopter. Blue Lake is quite a popular fishing spot due to the lack of fishing lakes in this area, so be prepared for company on the weekends and holidays.

There are a few campsites located at various spots around the lake. You'll find many fire pits near the water, but please don't use them. Lakeshore vegetation has been badly damaged due to inconsiderate folks camping too close to shore.

If you're heading to Gearhart Mountain, follow the trail to the southwest end of the lake at 3.1 miles. Head down the fairly level trail and at 3.9 miles you'll reach Gearhart Marsh.

While crossing the marsh be sure to look for Rocky Mountain elk, especially during the summer and fall months, when a herd of about 30 to 50 animals wander in and out of the area.

Continue up the trail at a moderate grade. At 4.7 miles the trail curves and heads south. At 6.7 miles you'll reach the junction of the Gearhart Trail No. 100 and the Boulder Spring Trail No. 100A. At this point you may want to walk over to the east side of the ridge for a nice view of the surrounding wilderness and the Gearhart Marsh.

The next 0.5 mile is an easy hike to the high point along the Gearhart Trail. From this vantage point, at 8,040 feet, there is a grand view of the Notch at 8,364 feet.

(If you want to continue your hike to the southern boundary of the Gearhart Wilderness you'll find #2, CORRAL CREEK TRAILHEAD TO THE NOTCH most helpful.)

The Notch, Gearhart Mountain

INTRODUCTION TO THE GRASSY KNOB WILDERNESS

The Grassy Knob Wilderness is located in the Coast Range, a few miles east of Port Orford, Oregon, and less than ten miles from the Pacific Ocean. Established as a Wilderness with the passage of the Oregon Wilderness Act of 1984, Grassy Knob came to be primarily to protect the immensely valuable anadromous fishery.

Extremely steep and rugged, the Wilderness consists of 17,200 acres managed by the Siskiyou National Forest. The area is also thickly forested. Several rocky bluffs provide but a few openings from which the Wilderness can be observed. As a result, few humans will ever see much of the area, rich in some very large and majestic old growth forests of Port Orford cedar, Douglas fir, hemlock and western red cedar.

Elevation ranges from a low of 100 feet on the Elk River, located in the southern portion of the Wilderness to a high of 2,474 feet atop Anvil Mountain, located near the heart of the wilderness.

Creeks and streams drain into two highly scenic coastal streams, the Elk River and Dry Creek. Steep-sided gorges, clear water, along with good salmon and steelhead fishing, make the streams quite popular, especially in the fall and spring, when the anadromous fish return to spawn in the river and its tributaries.

Three nesting pair of spotted owls have been found, but biologists believe there may be more, as the Grassy Knob Wilderness provides ideal old growth habitat for these medium-sized, dark-eyed owls, whose doglike barks and cries penetrate deep into the Wilderness.

Before Grassy Knob was designated Wilderness two roads were built to and into the area. Now the roads are closed at the boundary and serve as trails. The only true trail is the one leading to the site of the old Grassy Knob Lookout. (See guide: #4, GRASSY KNOB TRAIL.)

Today the lookout is gone, but the view is quite nice. From this point it's possible to see the surrounding pine-covered mountains, as well as waves breaking on the beautiful pacific coastline.

The lookout was removed in the sixties because other lookouts were able to cover the area much better. A bit of interesting history surrounds the lookout at Grassy Knob. During World War II, a plane, launched from a Japanese submarine, flew inland. It was seen from two lookouts, one of which was Grassy Knob. Some even say the Japanese aircraft was shot at from the lookout. Oregon author, Bert Webber, gives a full account of the unusual event in his book entitled, *Retaliation*.

The steep and rugged terrain associated with the Grassy Knob Wilderness may be difficult to hike in, but it can be viewed easily from the top of Grassy Knob. And because the area gets little use each hiker should be able to enjoy the view in comparative solitude.

For more information contact:

Siskiyou National Forest
Powers Ranger District
Powers, OR 97466
(503) 439-3011

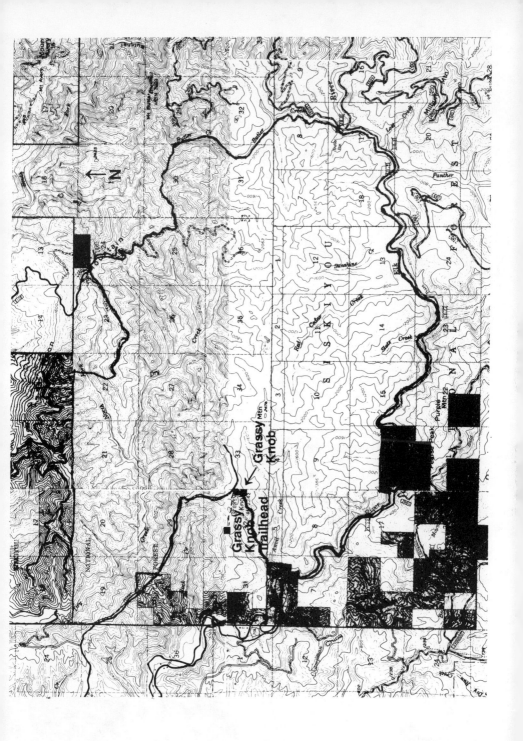

4 GRASSY KNOB TRAIL

Distance: 1.0 mile
Elevation gain: 150 feet; loss: 150 feet
High point: 2,342 feet
Usually open: All year
Topographic map: U.S.G.S. Port Orford, Oregon
15′   1954
Obtain map from: U.S.G.S. Denver, Colorado

Grassy Knob Wilderness is a land of steep terrain and thick understory. But an easy hike to the top of Grassy Knob will provide a grand view of the surrounding peaks, valleys, and the Pacific Ocean.

To reach the Wilderness drive north of Port Orford on U.S. Hwy. 101. Head east on Grassy Knob Rd. (Curry County Road No. 196), located three miles north of Port Orford. The road is paved for the first four miles then turns to a well-maintained gravel road. When pavement turns to gravel, take FS Road No. 5105 until it ends at 8.0 miles. A barricade prevents vehicles from driving farther up the road.

The trail is located at the east end of the parking area. A sign is posted to point you in the right direction. Cross the barricade and follow the road until it begins to level off, about 0.5 mile. Just before you reach the crest, head up the bank to the right. The trail is unmarked but there is a cut in the bank which should tip you off. The trail leads to the southwest for 50 feet or so, then to the southeast for another 50 feet. Once you reach this point the trail is easy to find. Follow it 150 yards to the top of Grassy Knob. From this point there is a 180 degree view.

To continue the one mile hike to the end of the road, hike back to the road and over the crest. The road consists of gradual ups and downs and is an easy hike. There are a few spots where you can get a good view of the surrounding area, but vegetation obscures the view for the most part.

Spotted owl

INTRODUCTION TO THE KALMIOPSIS WILDERNESS

Hikers who crave variety will find the Kalmiopsis Wilderness a most intriguing place. There is the Kalmiopsis leachiana, a rare plant for which the wilderness is named, the chance for a memorable hike to the top of Bald Mountain, the opportunity for a short hike across rocky, serpentine soil to Vulcan Lake, and more.

The Kalmiopsis Wilderness is located in southwest Oregon, approximately 30 miles east of the coastal town of Brookings. Straddling the Siskiyou Mountains of the Klamath Mountain Range, just north of the Oregon-California border, the wilderness reaches from a low elevation of 500 feet near the Illinois River to 5,098 feet atop Pearsoll Peak.

The Siskiyou National Forest manages the 179,862 acrea area. Managing the Wilderness includes maintaining 153 miles of existing trail. Also, there are 21.5 miles of old mining road which are used as trails. The trails are maintained on a rotating basis, with each trail usually worked every three to five years. A decrease in spending prevents yearly maintenance.

One of the least known and least visited wilderness areas, the Kalmiopsis Wilderness was originally designated a primitive area in 1946. At that time a total of 76,900 acreas was set aside. Eighteen years later, on September 3, 1964, the area became a unit of the National Wilderness Preservation System and came to be called the Kalmiopsis Wilderness. With the passage of the Endangered American Wilderness Act of 1978, the Kalmiopsis was expanded to its current size.

One advantage to hiking the Kalmiopsis is the constant change of scenery. There are deep canyons, rocky ridges, grand vistas, serpentine slopes, crystal clear streams, rivers to fish and play in, and seven small lakes to explore. Because of the extremely rugged terrain, be prepared to do a fair amount of climbing and descending. The Forest Service claims to have heard unverified rumors about some of the steep trails. One in particular, the Pupps Camp Way Trail, repeatedly has caused those carrying packs down the trail "to shrink a full 12-inches in height" by the time they reach the bottom of the trail.

The Kalmiopis Wilderness is often called a "botanists paradise" and with good reason. Recognized as having the largest variety of plant species any place in Oregon, you'll find such rare plants as the pre-ice age shrub the Kalmiopsis leachiana. First discovered near Gold Basin in 1930, the Wilderness was later named after this unique treasure. The oldest surviving member of the heath family, the Kalmiopsis flower usually blooms in May or June and resembles a tiny, delicate wild rose, or a miniature rhododendron. Found almost exclusively within the boundaries of the Kalmiopsis Wilderness, the Kalmiopsis leachiana grows nowhere else in the world except for one small patch in the Cascade Mountains of Oregon and four sites just outside the Kalmiopsis Wilderness boundary.

There are other species to observe when hiking into the Kalmiopsis. There is the Brewer spruce, a rare American spruce, also known as a weeping spruce, with long, stiff, drooping branches. Also, there are such beautiful and interesting plants as the rhododendron, azalea, lady's slipper and the insect eating California pitcher plant. In addition, the wilderness holds the possibility of species undiscovered and unnamed, and lures botanists and flower enthusiasts alike to view the approximately 1,000 plant species found here. Please remember that plant collecting is prohibited.

Although black bear, deer, and elk inhabit the Wilderness along with many other species of animal and bird life, wildlife populations are not tremendous. The harsh environment found in the Kalmiopsis limits the amount of suitable habitat. Still, if you are lucky you may just see a doe and her fawn tiptoeing into your camp, or maybe you'll see a black bear running across one of the prairies on Bald Mountain. If not, there is plenty else to see and do.

Mining relics can be seen in many parts of the Kalmiopsis. Drawn to the area in the 1850's, prospectors came with the dream of cashing in the huge gold nuggets they hoped to find. Nearby towns shot up overnight. They prospered, and later they died. Once old miners' routes, the trails are now followed by those trying to gain a sense of peace and serenity found in the Kalmiopsis Wilderness.

Today's visitors can experience a bit of the past by viewing such relics as the mines themselves, rusty tools, cable, pans, old cabins, and sometimes an old cabin foundation. Along with gold mines, chromes mines were also worked, but only until the 1950's. Today, a few valid gold mines are still being worked, but only with an approved operating plan. Mining is allowed in the Wilderness per the National Wilderness Preservation System Act of 1964.

Fishing is another activity that can be pursued in the Kalmiopsis. The major streams have runs of anadromous fish which include winter steelhead, cutthroat, and fall chinook salmon. Fishing is not the best during the summer months. Fish during the fall and late winter months for the better runs.

Now that all the advantages of hiking the Kalmiopsis have been explored there are a few inconveniences to make note of. First, there are rattlesnakes in the Kalmiopsis, and scorpions too. Watch where you place your hands and feet. Also, poison oak can be found in many areas, particularly at lower elevations along the Illinois and Chetco Rivers. And persons allergic to insect stings should note that yellowjackets and hornets inhabit the Wilderness, increasing in numbers as summer progresses.

Spring and fall are the most pleasant times to visit the Kalmiopsis as the summer months tend to be extremely hot and dry. Water is perhaps the biggest problem for summer travelers. Scarce on ridgetops, water can be found in the larger rivers, creeks, and streams, but may be available only in their lower reaches during late summer. For those that prefer hiking in the hot summer months please note which water sources are available all year-round. And for up-to-date water information contact the Siskiyou National Forest.

With a bit of thought and the necessary preparations, a visit to the Kalmiopsis can be a truly rewarding experience. Rare and unusual plants, wildlife, solitude, and rugged wild country combine to make this wilderness the perfect spot for the backpacker who doesn't care for crowds.

For more information contact the following:

Chetco Ranger District
555 Fifth St.
Brookings, OR 97415
(503) 469-2196

or

Galice Ranger District
Post Office Building
P.O. Box 1131
Grants Pass, OR 97526
(503) 476-3830

or

Gold Beach Ranger District
1225 S. Ellensburg, Box 7
Gold Beach, OR 97444
(503) 247-6651

or

Illinois Valley Ranger District
26468 Redwood Hwy.
Cave Junction, OR. 97523
(503) 592-2166

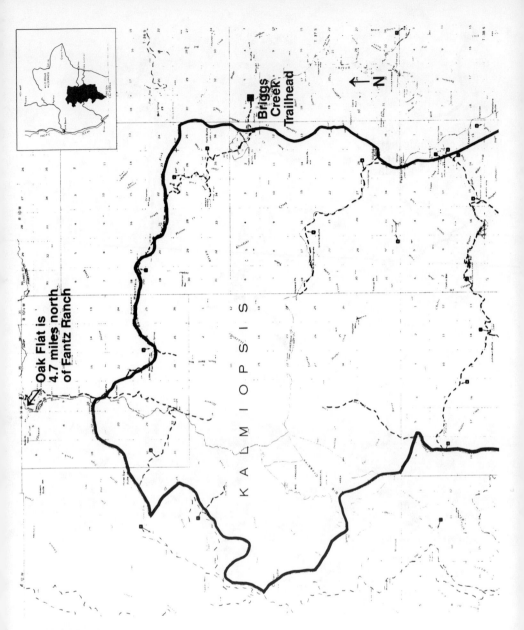

Briggs Creek Trailhead

Oak Flat is 4.7 miles north of Fantz Ranch

K A L M I O P S I S

Northern Section

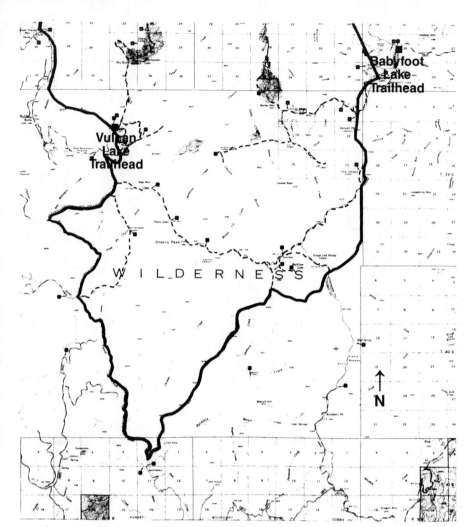

Southern Section

5

VULCAN LAKE TRAILHEAD
to VULCAN LAKE
to GARDNER MINE LOOP

Distance: 3.1 miles
Elevation gain: 900 feet; loss: 800 feet
High point: 4,100 feet
Usually open: May through October
Topographic map: Kalmiopsis Wilderness
**   Map**
Obtain map from: Siskiyou National Forest

A hike to Vulcan Lake will provide each person with an introduction into the vast and rugged world of the Kalmiopsis Wilderness. Hike over rocky terrain, passing twisted pines along the way, then drop down to Vulcan Lake, a great spot for an overnight trip or a day hike. Also, visit Little Vulcan Lake and the remains of Gardner Mine.

To reach the Vulcan Lake Trailhead, head east on North Bank Road (County Road No. 784), located off Hwy. 101 just south of the coast town of Brookings, Oregon. The paved road follows along the Chetco River for a few miles, turning into FS Road No. 1376 at 10.6 miles.

At 14.0 miles the road turns into a well maintained gravel road. At 16.4 miles turn right onto FS Road No. 1909. Turn right again at 18.0 miles, staying on the same road. At 26.0 miles reach a fork in the road. Head left. Pass Red Mountain Prairie campsite at 29.0 miles. There is a picnic table, fire pit, and outhouse, along with spring water located across the road. Continue on, passing FS Road No. 260 which leads to the Chetco Divide Trail / Vulcan Peak Trail-

head at 29.7 miles. Reach the Vulcan Lake Trailhead at 31.5 miles. There is another picnic area located at the trailhead, complete with picnic table and outhouse.

Please sign in at the registration box before entering the Wilderness. For your convenience, trash bags are also located at the registration box. Please pack out whatever you pack in!

Enter the Wilderness a few yards from the trailhead while hiking an old jeep road, Johnson Butte Trail No. 1110. Reach a fork in the trail shortly thereafter. Head to the right, hiking Vulcan Lake Trail No. 1110A, gradually climbing over red, rocky terrain. Notice the gnarled pines, western azaleas, and the countless opportunities for wonderful views while you hike.

At 1.0 mile reach the high point on this hike. From here you'll get a tremendous view of Vulcan Lake, Vulcan Peak, and Red Mountain to the south. Descend across the open slope, switching back to the left as you near Vulcan Lake. The trail forks at 1.3 miles. Turn right and arrive at Vulcan Lake at 1.4 miles.

Vulcan Peak provides a nice backdrop to Vulcan Lake. (The 4,655 foot peak can be climbed via another trail located off FS Road No. 260.) At Vulcan Lake the best campsites are found on the north end of the lake. Walk along the ridge east of the lake for another view of the valley below.

To continue on, head back to the trail, turn right, and hike a hundred yards to another fork. Turn right on the signed "Trail" and gradually to moderately descend to Little Vulcan Lake at 1.6 miles. There is little in the way of campsites here, but a lot in the way of plants. Notice all of the Darlingtonia or California pitcher plants. Found in meadows and boggy areas rich in water-logged acid soils, these unusual plants are unique in that they trap and digest insects.

Head back to the main trail at 1.7 miles to continue on to Gardner Mine. Turn right, gradually climbing along the rocky trail. At 2.0 miles begin a gradual descent to a small waterhole. Cross to the north end of the waterhole, now hiking an old mining road to Gardner Mine at 2.2 miles. (There is a spur trail off the road just prior to the mine. Be sure to stick to the road.)

The Gardner Mine Road was built in the 1940's by Fred Gardner. Between 1952 and 1958 the area was mined for chromite (chrome). In the GEOLOGY AND MINERAL RESOURCE OF THE UPPER CHETCO DRAINAGE AREA, OREGON, Bulletin 88, Len Ramps writes, "The largest production of high grade lump ore from a single occurence was about 200 long tons from the Gardner mine." See the old mine shaft to your left as you continue hiking the road to the junction of the Johnson Butte Trail No. 1110 at 2.5 miles.

Turn left, gradually descending via an old mine road, then remaining fairly level to the trailhead at 3.1 miles.

View north from the Vulcan Lake Trail

SOUTHERN OREGON WILDERNESS AREAS

View east from Vulcan Lake

Gardner Mine

SOUTHERN OREGON WILDERNESS AREAS

6

VULCAN LAKE TRAILHEAD to BOX CANYON CAMP

Distance: 10.5 miles
Elevation gain: 1,100 feet; loss: 3,700 feet
High point: 3,900 feet
Usually open: May through October
Topographic map: Kalmiopsis Wilderness
                               Map
Obtain map from: Siskiyou National Forest

This trip will reward each hiker with wide views from atop rocky ridges. And in the spring admire the extremely rare Kalmiopsis leachiana found along sections of this trail. Later, descend through old growth forest to Box Canyon Creek and a nice spot to camp. Those with a shuttle available may want to end their hike at the Babyfoot Lake Trailhead. (Please see #7 BABYFOOT LAKE TRAILHEAD TO BOX CANYON CAMP for instructions.)

To reach the Vulcan Lake Trailhead drive east on North Bank Road (County Road No. 784), located off Hwy. 101, just south of the coastal town of Brookings, Oregon. The paved road follows the north bank of the Chetco River for a few miles, turning into FS Road No. 1376 at 10.6 miles.

At 14.0 miles the road turns from paved to well-maintained gravel. Turn right onto FS Road No. 1909 at 16.4 miles and at 18.0 miles turn right again, staying on the same road. The road forks at 26.0 miles. Head left. Pass the Red Mountain Prairie Campsite at 29.0 miles. There is a picnic table, fire pit, outhouse, and a spring located across the road. Reach the Chetco Divide Trail/ Vulcan Peak turnoff (FS Road No. 260) at 29.7 miles. Continue past the turnoff, reaching the Vulcan Lake Trailhead at 31.5 miles. Again, there is a picnic area complete with picnic table and outhouse.

Please sign in at the registration box located at the trailhead. For your convenience, trash bags are also available at the registration site. Please pack out whatever you pack in!

Enter the Wilderness a few yards from the trailhead. Hike along the old jeep road, Johnson Butte Trail No. 1110, staying left when the trail splits. The side trail to your right leads to Vulcan Lake.

Continue down the road, remaining level for nearly 0.3 mile before gradually climbing to a junction at 0.6 mile. The trail to the right leads to Gardner Mine. Continue north on the Johnson Butte Trail, gradually descending through the forest. Rhododendrons brighten up the forest in the spring, their brilliant pink flowers a real treat indeed. At 1.4 miles look for a patch of Kalmiopsis leachiana on the east side of the trail.

From this point climb gradually to moderately, reaching a high point at 2.0 miles. The view from here is wonderful as you hike along a narrow saddle. Continue climbing across an open ridge where you'll see more leachiana, in addition to iris and other wildflowers in the spring. Cross the west slope of Dry Butte at 2.9 miles then begin a level or slight descent past a burned-out area where you'll see knobcone pines. At 4.0 miles the trail curves to the west. Notice Valen Lake down the mountain to the northeast.

The trail continues past more leachiana and rhododendrons as you gradually hike up and down to a ridgetop and a sign "water" at 5.2 miles, referring to Salamander Lake. Just over the ridge, on the south side, is a campsite with a flat spot for a tent and a fire pit. If you'd like to visit Salamander Lake continue down the trail, dropping 300 to 400 feet on a steep trail to the lily-pad filled lake.

Back on the main trail, gradually climb to a point where the trail now heads west at 6.0 miles. Descend gradually to 6.6 miles and another "water" sign. This narrow trail is moderately steep, leading to two small campsites, approximately 200 to 300 feet down the trail. One site is located before the spring, one after the spring. The trail leads directly to the cold water, which flows all summer. Rhododendrons and azaleas line the trail for a special treat.

Soon after passing the "water" sign, climb gradually to 7.0 miles through a lush forest of trees and ferns, then descend to a junction at 7.5 miles.

A sign at the junction points left to "Cedar Camp." Head this way to Windy Camp, a nearby camp without a view, but there is a flat area for a tent, a fire pit, and a small spring (really small) just east of the camp near the sign "water." Cedar Camp is located about two miles farther down the trail.

To reach Box Canyon turn right at the junction, heading towards Taggarts Bar via Upper Chetco Trail No. 1102. During the next few miles the trail decends at a gradual to moderate rate, sometimes dropping at a steep angle, also, but mostly it is moderate. Pass through old growth forest which includes Douglas fir and sugar pine, with a lush understory in some sections. Before reaching Box Canyon, the trail switchbacks down to Box Canyon Creek at 10.5 miles.

There are two campsites near each side of the creek. Before reaching the creek, notice the camp on the north side of the drainage. It's located just off the trail on a bluff overlooking Box Canyon Creek. To reach the second campsite, hike down to the creek, cross carefully (you must ford the creek as there isn't a bridge), then hike up the trail on the south side.

Box Canyon Creek

SOUTHERN OREGON WILDERNESS AREAS

er Creek

Crossing the Chetco River

7 BABYFOOT LAKE TRAIL-HEAD to BABYFOOT LAKE to BOX CANYON CAMP

Distance: 18.2 miles
Elevation gain: 3,150 feet; loss: 5,850 feet
High point: 4,600 feet
Usually open: May through October
Topographic map: Kalmiopsis Wilderness Map
Obtain map from: Siskiyou National Forest

Babyfoot Lake is a popular spot for many folks, and one spot that hikers who desire solitude will want to avoid. But there are plenty of wide open spaces for those individuals who plan to hike to Box Canyon. And those lucky enough to have a shuttle may want to continue on from Box Canyon, hiking up to Johnson Butte and out via the Vulcan Lake Trailhead. (See #6 VULCAN LAKE TRAILHEAD TO BOX CANYON CAMP for details.)

To reach the Babyfoot Lake Trailhead drive U.S. Hwy. 199 to FS Road No. 4201, located five miles north of Cave Junction, Oregon. Head west on the well-maintained gravel road for approximately 17 miles. Turn left on FS Road No. 140, reaching the trailhead in one-half mile.

From the large parking area, hike past the registration sign and box (please sign in first) and enter the forest. It's a gradual up and down hike to the junction of Babyfoot Lake/ Canyon Peak trails at 0.3 mile. Turn right and hike, again up and down, winding around the mountainside to Babyfoot Lake at 1.2 miles. Enter the Wilder-

ness just prior to reaching the lake. There are quite a few campsites to choose from. Also, there are plenty of fire pits. Please don't make any new ones. And anglers, please note: the fishing is not the greatest at Babyfoot Lake.

Notice the rare Brewer spruce, a weeping pine, as you walk around the lake. At the north end of the lake, hike past some small trees and catch a trail heading north. Follow this trail through the trees as it climbs gradually to an old road at 1.7 miles. (There are a couple of short, but steep up and downs just before reaching the road.) Turn left and follow the road, gradually hiking up and down through the trees.

Continue to 3.2 miles and another trail which heads to Babyfoot Lake. Stay on the road and gradually descend to the junction of the Little Chetco/W. Fork Canyon Trails at 4.8 miles.

Again, keep to the old mining road. As you hike from the junction to an old mine at 5.5 miles, be aware that two trails intersect the main road. The first trail is not a big problem as it isn't too noticeable. Stay right and don't leave the road. Just before reaching the mine there is a road heading off to the right and above the road you are walking. Keep to the left.

There are plenty of rusty tools around the mine, and a small cabin is built on stilts near the road. There is an old outhouse and a doughboy swimming pool which appears to be some type of water reservoir for the miners. Also, there is spring water near the mine.

Descend gradually along the open road then climb to a large open serpentine area at 6.8 miles. Trees grow here and there on the rocky soil and the view is magnificent. See Vulcan Peak, Red Mountain, Chetco Peak, Canyon Peak and more.

Continue along the road to 7.0 miles. There is a trail heading off to the west at this point. Turn right on the trail and gradually descend along the semi-open slope to Bailey Cabin at 8.3 miles. Look for leachiana flowers along this trail during May and June, the time when they are most likely to be in bloom. There are a few nice campsites in the vicinity of the cabin. Don't expect to sleep in the cabin, though, as it has collapsed and nearly all of the roof now lays on the ground. There is a pond and creek water nearby.

Climb gradually from the cabin. Reach the junction of Emily Cabin at 8.5 miles. Continue straight and to the west. At times there are wonderful views to the north where you'll see deep valleys and mountain peaks. A short distance farther and you'll see another view, only this time you're looking south to Chetco Peak, Red Mountain, and the mountain ranges beyond.

Reach the northeast side of Bailey Mountain at 8.8 miles. There is a nice campsite on the saddle with a flat site for a tent.

To continue to Box Canyon, descend moderately through a forest of old growth trees where rhododendrons and azaleas brighten up the trail. Also there are more opportunities to view Kalmiopsis. There are a few gradual up and downs before reaching a sign for "Sowell Spring" at 9.7 miles. The spring is located 200 feet to the right and down the slope.

Reach another spring at 9.9 miles. Signed "Bumby Spring" is about 25 feet down the slope and has Darlingtonia, or the California pitcher plant growing near it.

From Bumby Spring, descend moderately (sometimes steep) to the southern Carter Creek Camp at 10.7 miles. The campsite is located on the west side of the trail and is easy to see. Walk to the edge of the camp for a view of the Chetco River below. Carter Creek is located just north of the campsite. And it's an easy hike down to the creek for water.

There is another campsite on the north side of Carter Creek. To reach this site, ford Carter Creek, then hike up the small incline until the trail levels off. As the trail curves to the right a bit look for a flat area to the left. This site is under the trees and not as open as the southern site. Also, there is more poison oak near this camp.

To continue on to Box Canyon follow the trail past the north Carter Creek Camp, hiking gradual up and downs through the trees. Descend moderately to the Chetco River at 12.0 miles. The trail passes a sign "Blake's Bar" when you reach the rocky shore of the Chetco. Those hiking from the opposite way (Box Canyon to Babyfoot) will find the sign most helpful in picking up the trail after crossing the river.

Ford the Chetco River with care. At times it is too high to permit a safe crossing. Please check with the Forest Service for a current update on the river. The trail begins again about 100 yards downstream from where you emerged near Blake's Bar.

Climb the switchbacks then climb through the trees to a creek at 12.2 miles. From here the trail gradually gains and descends while crossing a slope above the river. At 12.5 miles the trail meets with a dirt road. Sign "Bailey Mountain Trail No. 1109" at this point.

Turn right, hiking the road as it follows the river, descending to a junction at 13.6 miles. Chetco Pass is located to the right. To reach Box Canyon head to the left, hiking Upper Chetco Trail No. 1102 now. The trail is a series of ups and downs, again through the trees with some

good views of the river. Reach another junction for Chetco Pass at 13.9 miles. Head to the left.

Again it's an up and down hike to a grand view at 14.0 miles. See Pearsoll Peak to the northeast. At 5,098 feet, Pearsoll Peak is the highest peak in the Wilderness. To the northwest see Tincup Peak, Heather Mountain and the Chetco River drainage below.

The trail heads to the west now, climbing and descending at a gradual to moderate rate on semi-open slope and through the forest. There are some good views of the river as you hike this stretch. Cross one stream at 14.9 miles and another at 15.4 miles. Look for California lady's slipper, maiden hair fern, and more.

Climb moderately, then level off with some ups and downs, crossing another small stream at 16.0 miles. Hike level then decend moderately to another dirt road at 16.3 miles. A sign and rock cairn mark the trail.

Descend at a moderate to steep grade down the road to Taggarts Bar Camp and a spring at 16.7 miles. Continue down the road and reach a junction at 16.8 miles. To reach the Chetco River hike down the road a few hundred yards. Turn left at the rock cairn and head through the grass to another campsite under the trees.

Climb the moderate to steep slope to the top of a ridge at 17.7 miles. Descend now on the moderate to steep grade, reaching the east side Box Canyon Camp at 18.3 miles.

There are two campsites near Box Canyon Creek. The east side camp is the first you'll come to before heading down the bluff to the creek. There is a fire pit, room for a tent, and all the water you need at the creek. Ford the creek and climb up the opposite bluff on the west side of the creek for another campsite.

8 BABYFOOT LAKE TRAIL-HEAD to BABYFOOT LAKE

Distance: 1.2 miles
Elevation gain: 200 feet; loss: 100 feet
High point: 4,400 feet
Usually open: May through October
Topographic map: Kalmiopsis Wilderness Map
Obtain map from: Siskiyou National Forest

Babyfoot Lake is an easy hike for those folks who would like to visit the Wilderness, but don't want to hike in a long ways to do so. Because of its accessibility though, Babyfoot Lake is sometimes overcrowded. Hikers who desire solitude will want to avoid this area. But there are some positive reasons for visiting it. There are many species of unique plant life in this protected botanical area. And who can resist camping near the waters of a Wilderness lake?

To reach the Babyfoot Lake Trailhead drive U.S. Hwy. 199 to FS Road No. 4201 located five miles north of Cave Junction, Oregon. Head west on the well-maintained gravel road for approximately 17 miles. Turn left on FS Road No. 140, reaching the trailhead in one-half mile.

Babyfoot Lake

From the large parking area, hike past the registration sign and box (please sign in first) and enter the forest. It's a gradual up and down hike to the junction of Babyfoot Lake / Canyon Peak trails at 0.3 mile. Turn right and hike, again up and down, winding around the mountainside to Babyfoot Lake at 1.2 miles. There are quite a few campsites to choose from around the lake. Also, there are plenty of fire pits. Please don't make any new ones.

As you hike around the lake notice the weeping pines called Brewer Spruce which have long, drooping branches, as well as a jigsaw-patterned bark which is an off-white color.

The Forest Service has informed me that although Babyfoot Lake was stocked at one time, it isn't stocked at the present time so the fishing may not be the best. Of course, it doesn't hurt to throw in your line and see if you can get a nibble or two.

9 BRIGGS CREEK TRAILHEAD to BALD MOUNTAIN LOOKOUT

Distance: 11.9 miles
Elevation gain: 3,203 feet; loss: 257 feet
High point: 4,000 feet
Usually open: May through October
Topographic map: Kalmiopsis Wilderness Map
Obtain map from: Siskiyou National Forest

In this guidebook you'll find two detailed hikes to the top of Bald Mountain. Both hikes begin from points called Oak Flat. One is the Oak Flat near Briggs Creek (Briggs Creek Trailhead) and is located to the southeast of Bald Mountain. The other is the Oak Flat near Nancy Creek (Oak Flat Trailhead) and is located to the northwest of Bald Mountain. Both are excellent hikes. Those with a shuttle may want to begin at one trailhead, climb the mountain, and descend via the opposite trail.

To reach the Briggs Creek Trailhead, drive County Road No. 5070 (Illinois Valley Rd.) from Selma, Oregon, located off U.S. Hwy. 199. At 6.7 miles the road turns into FS Road No. 4103. The road forks at 11.6 miles. Remain on FS Road No. 4103. The road changes from paved to well-maintained gravel, and then to gravel with limited maintenance before reaching the trailhead at 18.3 miles. Although rough in spots, the road is still passable in most passenger cars, except those with low clearance.

Briggs Creek Campground is located at the trailhead. There are picnic tables, outhouses, fire pits, and the sound of Briggs Creek nearby.

To begin hiking to Pine Flat, cross Briggs Creek via a bridge then hike a series of gradual ups and downs along the semi-open slope to Panther Creek at 0.5 mile. At 1.0 mile enter the Wilderness. Continue on to a campsite at 2.0 miles. It's easy to obtain water at this campsite for Hayden Creek is but a short distance down the trail. The York Creek Botanical Area also begins at this point.

Again, gradually hike up and down to York Creek at 2.4 miles, and cross another creek at 2.5 miles. Hike through the trees shortly thereafter, gradually climbing, then back out onto the semi-open slope and a wonderful view of the Illinois River. Continue climbing to 3.0 miles then begin a gradual descent through the trees to Clear Creek at 4.2 miles. The Forest Service claims that Clear Creek may have the clearest water in the world. Lacking any siltation whatsoever, this tiny waterfall is nearly transparent. A campsite is located just up the hill from the creek.

Continue through the trees, hiking a gradual up and down to the junction of Pine Flat Trail No. 1219 and Illinois River Trail No. 1162 at 5.1 miles. Pine Flat Trail leads to Pine Flat, a great spot for camping and relaxing and a descent of nearly 1,000 feet to the river. (See #11 BRIGGS CREEK TO PINE FLAT for details.)

To reach Bald Mountain, turn right at the junction and continue on Illinois River Trail. Hike the level trail for a ways then descend through the trees to East Fork Pine Creek at 6.6 miles. Climb from the creek then gradually descend again to West Fork Pine Creek at 7.1 miles. About 50 feet after crossing the creek, a side trail climbs to a level campsite above it.

Climb moderately to a small knoll at 7.6 miles. There is also a campsite here, although the nearest water is at West Fork Pine Creek. Gradually climb to 7.9 miles and a view of Chinaman Hat Peak to the north. At 8.6 miles the trail levels off.

Reach a fork in the trail at 8.9 miles. The old trail heads off to the right, and the new trail is on the left. The old trail provides another great view of Chinaman Hat Peak and the forest beyond. But a logging road, cut close to the Wilderness boundary, obscures the otherwise beautiful view. The new trail was built for those who would rather avoid the sight of logging roads.

Also, many hikers will notice the wire strung out along the trail leading to Bald Mountain and down the west side of the mountain, as well. At one time the telephone cable found here linked the Bald Mountain Lookout with points beyond. Because the cable has historical significance, most of it will remain as it is. Some portions will be removed and saved.

From this point, gradually climb, entering old growth ponderosa pine, Douglas fir, madrone, and black oak forest. Reach the junction of Florence Way / Bald Mountain at 9.7 miles. Soon after this junction the trail climbs at a steep grade as you wind around to the north side of Bald Mountain. Later the trail moderately climbs.

Reach nearly level ground and the south side of the mountain at 11.6 miles. Continue on to Bald Mountain Camp at 11.9 miles.

Before reaching the camp there are two separate trails leading to the Bald Mountain Lookout. Bald Mountain Camp is near the second trail leading to the top of the mountain. The spring and camp are easy to find as the trail passes directly over the spring water and the camp is located just a hundred feet or so from the spring. If the Bald Mountain Camp is occupied there is another camp down the hill via a well-worn trail.

Bald Mountain Lookout is easy to locate. Just follow the trails up the mountain to the highest point at about 4,000 feet. On the site of the old lookout, which was burned down by the Forest Service, the view is fantastic. On a super clear day see the summit of Mt. Shasta, the Klamath Mountains, the Siskiyou Mountains, and the Pacific Ocean.

View south from Bald Mountain Lookout

10 OAK FLAT TRAILHEAD to BALD MOUNTAIN LOOKOUT

Distance: 16.2 miles
Elevation gain: 5,586 feet; loss: 1,820 feet
High point: 4,000 feet
Usually open: May through October
Topographic map: Kalmiopsis Wilderness Map
Obtain map from: Siskiyou National Forest

You'll find two guides to hiking to the top of Bald Mountain in this book with both hikes beginning from points called Oak Flat. One is the Oak Flat near Nancy Creek (Oak Flat Trailhead) and is located to the northwest of Bald Mountain. Both are excellent hikes to the top of the mountain. Those with a shuttle may want to begin at one trailhead, climb Bald Mountain, and descend via the opposite trail.

To reach the Oak Flat Trailhead from the coastal and river town of Gold Beach, Oregon, drive County Road No. 595, following along the south bank of the famous Rogue River. Later Road No. 595 turns into FS Road No. 33. At 26.6 miles from Hwy. 101, just past the Illinois River Bridge, turn right on County Road No. 450. Drive another 3.2 miles on County Road 450 to the trailhead.

From the large parking area head south along the Illinois River Trail No. 1162, remaining mostly level to the bridge over Nancy Creek at 0.8 mile. Continue on through the trees, climbing very gradually and crossing four more creeks by 1.5 miles.

Gradually climb to Buzzards Roost at 2.5 miles. Obtain a nice view of the Illinois River from Buzzards Roost by climbing out onto the rocks. From this point gradually descend through the forest then out onto a semi-open slope adorned with madrones and azaleas. Also, notice the Canyon Live Oak and the White Oak as you hike from Oak Flat to Bald Mountain.

Reach a junction at 3.8 miles. The Illinois River Trail continues to the right. Straight ahead is a trail leading to Indian Flat, a nice spot to camp. Located about 0.5 mile to the east, it is near the confluence of two creeks, the North Fork and the Indigo.

Switchback down the moderate grade to Indigo Creek at 4.0 miles. Just before reaching the creek there is a trail leading off to the east. This trail also leads to Indian Flat. Anglers may catch steelhead in Indigo Creek.

Cross Indigo Creek by bridge then climb the moderate switchbacks to the junction of Silver Peak/Hobson Horn Trail No. 1166 at 4.7 miles. There is a sign nearby, "Dogs on Leash." Descend gradually to another sign, "Dogs Running Will Be Shot," and a trail. This trail leads to the Fantz Ranch, private land which borders adjacent to the National Forest Land. They have livestock at their ranch and want to be sure that hikers keep their dogs under control.

Cross several more streams while descending through the forest. At 5.3 miles you'll see the Fantz Ranch on the west side of the trail. Cross another creek and another after that while hiking a series of up and down grades in a southwest direction.

Reach Black Rock Creek at 5.9 miles. Gradually climb up to another creek at 6.1 miles then it's a gradual up and down to Coon Creek at 6.5 miles and Bluff Creek at 7.0 miles. Water is available at these fern-covered creeks most of the year. Continue through the trees, eventually descending by switchback to Connors Place, a meadow with spring water located just across the trail. Connors Place is also the point where the trail enters into the Wilderness.

From Connors Place continue through the trees then out onto an open slope with views of the Illinois River. Notice some of the deep, blue pools of calm water. Descend gradually to Silver Creek at 8.6 miles. Fortunately, there is a bridge across this fast moving creek. Again, steelhead may be caught in Silver Creek.

Continue up the south side of the creek, climbing to a bluff with several nice campsites. The view couldn't be better from one of the bluff sites where you can see the crystal clear waters of Silver Creek merge with the deep, blue waters of the Illinois River. An almost constant breeze helps to keep down the mosquitoes.

To reach Bald Mountain, climb gradually to a junction at 9.1 miles. An interesting side trip is straight ahead on the Illinois River Trail and leads to Colliers Bar in 3.0 miles. It's a beautiful spot for camping, for admiring the steep walled canyon or the river, and for seeing and hearing the waterfalls that are found there.

Also, there is a campsite at the junction (Grapevine Camp) with creek water a few yards south on the Collier Bar Trail. The camps at Silver Creek are much better as there are fewer mosquitoes and the view is much more rewarding.

Turn left to reach Bald Mountain, climbing moderate switchbacks (sometimes steep) across the slope. There are many game trails here so be careful to remain on the main trail. At 10.2 miles the trail climbs moderately through the trees. Reach Little Bald Mountain Prairie at 12.5 miles. This is a wonderful spot for a picnic as there is a pleasant view, and it is a good spot to look for black bear in the spring.

As you hike along the Bald Mountain Trail you may wonder what all the wire is doing strung out along the trail. (This wire also runs down the east side of Bald Mountain.) Once this telephone wire linked the Bald Mountain Lookout with points beyond. Because the cable has historical significance most of the wire will remain. Those portions that are removed will be saved.

Continue climbing to Polar Spring Camp and Polar Spring at 13.0 miles. A few hundred yards farther up the trail and you'll come to the junction of Pupps Camp and South Bend Mountain. At this point there is another camp on the north side of the trail.

Gradually climb through the trees and open prairie. Reach a sign "Allen Cabin – Water, 1/8 mile" at 14.5 miles. We were unable to locate this cabin or water, but the Forest Service has informed us all that remains are pieces of the cabin, but water is located about 600 feet from the trail and about 150 feet from the cabin site. From the sign head southwest to south on the faint trail. Also there is a larger spring farther down the hill and to the east of the cabin site, but is more difficult to find.

Soon after reaching this sign cross through the Middle Bald Prairie then gradually climb to Bald Mountain Camp at 16.2 miles. The trails crosses over from the south side of the mountain to the north side and back to the south side again before reaching the camp.

There is a spring near the camp. In fact, the trail continues right over the spring. If the Bald Mountain Camp is occupied there is another camp down the hill via a well-worn trail.

The Bald Mountain Lookout is easy to locate. head across the stream and follow the sign "Bald Mountain Lookout" up the mountain to the highest point at about 4,000 feet. From the sight of the old lookout, which was burned down by the Forest Service, the view is fantastic. On a crystal clear day see Mt. Shasta, the Siskiyou mountains, the Klamath Mountains, and the mighty Pacific Ocean.

Illinois River

11 BRIGGS CREEK TRAILHEAD to PINE FLAT

Distance: 5.8 miles
Elevation gain: 903 feet; loss: 1,107 feet
High point: 1,651 feet
Usually open: May through October
Topographic map: Kalmiopsis Wilderness Map
Obtain map from: Siskiyou National Forest

The hike to Pine Flat from Briggs Creek is especially nice in the spring when wildflowers are blooming along the trail. There are many opportunities to observe a variety of flowers in the York Creek Botanical Area through which the trail passes. At the end of this hike, relax and enjoy the beautiful Illinois River.

To reach the Briggs Creek Trailhead drive County Road No. 5070 (Illinois Valley Rd.) from Selma, Oregon, located off U.S. Hwy. 199. At 6.7 miles the road turns into FS Road No. 4103.

The road forks at 11.6 miles. Remain on FS Road 4103. The road changes from paved to well-maintained gravel, and then to gravel with limited maintenance before reaching the trail head at 18.3 miles. Although the road is rough in spots, it is normally passable with a passenger car, except those with low clearance.

Briggs Creek Campground is located at the trailhead. There are picnic tables, outhouses, fire pits, and the sound of Briggs Creek nearby.

To begin hiking to Pine Flat, cross Briggs Creek via a bridge then hike a series of gradual ups and downs along the semi-open slope to Panther Creek at 0.5 mile. Enter the Wilderness at 1.0 mile. Continue on to a campsite at 2.0 miles. It's easy to obtain water at this campsite for Hayden Creek is but a short distance down the trail. The York Creek Botanical Area also begins at this point.

Again, gradually hike up and down to York Creek at 2.4 miles, and cross another creek at 2.5 miles. Hike through the trees shortly thereafter, gradually climbing then back out onto the semi-open slope and wonderful view of the Illinois River. Continue climbing to 3.0 miles then begin a gradual descent through the trees to Clear Creek at 4.2 miles. The Forest Service claims that the water here is perhaps the clearest in the world. Lacking any siltation whatsoever, the waters of this tiny waterfall are nearly transparent. Besides water, there is a camp just up the hill from the creek.

Continue through the trees, hiking a gradual up and down to the junction of Pine Flat Trail No. 1219 and Illinois River Trail No. 1162 at 5.1 miles. Head west (straight), descending a moderate to steep grade with some switchbacks near the top. Reach Pine Flat and level ground at 5.8 miles.

To the left are some nice campsites with easy access to the river. If you head to the right, cross a bridge over Pine Creek. There is another camp-site here. Continue through the trees until the trail leads to the rocky shore of the Illinois River. Scramble across the rocks, picking up the trail a short distance farther. This trail leads to Weaver Ranch, 0.3 mile from Pine Flat. Weaver Ranch is what you might expect—the site of an old homestead and a big flat area near the Illinois River. Those who like to explore will find farm machinery rusting in the tall grass.

Anglers will find the fishing poor in the summer, but fantastic along the Illinois River in late fall. Cast out your line and hook steelhead, coho salmon, and fall chinook. And swimmers will find deep, clear, water to swim in. What more could you ask for?

Illinois River from near Pine Flat

INTRODUCTION TO THE MOUNTAIN LAKES WILDERNESS

Mountain Lakes Wilderness has something for everyone. There are cold, clear lakes, high mountains, good fishing, deer, bald eagles, solitude, and much, much more.

Several million years ago a 12,000 foot massive composite volcano was "born" in the area which is now know as the Mountain Lakes Wilderness. The huge volcano covered roughly 85 square miles, making it one of the giants of the southern Cascades.

The mountain lost its status as "one of the giants" when the summit portion of the volcano collapsed into a huge crater or caldera. The same volcanic forces that once formed the mountain were now responsible for destroying it.

Later the earth cooled. Snow and ice gathered in the depths of the caldera forming glaciers which spilled over the rim and spread slowly down the sides of the mountain. Time passed. The caldera was reshaped as repeated glaciation combined with wind and water to tear at the mountain, leaving only fragments of the rim and portions of the base.

Mountain Lakes was first established as a primitive area in 1930 when the National Forest Service set aside 13,444 acres. This spectacular Wilderness has the distinction of being one of the first three primitive areas established in the Pacific Northwest Region. In 1940 Mountain Lakes was increased to its present size – 23,071 acres – and the area was renamed the Mountain Lakes Wild Area. With the passage of the Wilderness Act of 1964 the area was once again renamed and became a segment of the National Wilderness system.

Mountain Lakes Wilderness is located 15 airline miles northwest of Klamath Falls and 40 airline miles south of Crater Lake National Park. The Wilderness is managed by the Klamath Ranger District of the Winema National Forest.

Most of the Mountain Lakes Wilderness lies above 6,000 feet with Aspen Butte claiming the highest point in the Wilderness at 8,208 feet. The top of Aspen Butte can be reached by hiking along the ridge leading up to the Butte. Stunted trees line the ridge, their branches twisted in defiance, refusing to let go. Once on top, a 360 degree view will thrill all who make the climb. Mt. Shasta, Mt. McLoughlin, Upper Klamath Lake, and the Wilderness beyond are just a few of the spectacular sights one might see.

There are three maintained trails leading into the Mountain Lakes Wilderness. From the north, hike Varney Creek Trail No. 3713 and from the west hike Mountain Lakes Trail No. 3721. See the trail guide following this introduction for directions on reaching the Wilderness from the south entrance via Clover Creek Trail No. 3722. All three trails lead to the primary trail, Mountain Lakes Loop Trail No. 3727, which traces a 9.2 mile loop around the ancient caldera rim in the heart of the Wilderness.

Below 7,000 feet the trails wind through heavy stands of mountain hemlock mixed with Shasta red fir. At higher elevations the mountains are rich with alpine fir, white pine, and lodgepole pine. An occasional mountain meadow may also be found, particularly in the lower basins. During the spring and summer months brilliant wildflowers emerge to brighten the lengthening days of summer.

Mountain lakes are plentiful in the Wilderness with the majority of lakes found along the rim of the old crater. These lakes range in size from small ponds to good-size lakes such as Lake Harriette. With a surface of 70 acres, Lake Harriette is not only the largest lake in the Wilderness, but also the deepest. Its refreshing, blue waters reach a depth of 63 feet, and the swimming and fishing are out-of-this-world. Many of the larger Wilderness lakes are stocked with fish from time to time. Rainbow trout and brook trout are caught in most of the lakes.

Abundant wildlife adds to any wilderness experience. A variety of mammals, such as deer, bear, coyote, and bobcat live within the boundaries. And a wide variety of birds are commonly seen in the area, including bald eagles, osprey, owls, hawks, and numerous forest dwelling birds, like jays and nuthatches.

After snowmelt a few unpleasant creatures invade the area. Mosquitoes, gnats, and black flies can be expected in the early part of the season. After July, bugs are usually not a problem but carry insect repellent just in case.

As in all mountainous regions, the weather is always unpredictable. Frost can occur on any night throughout the summer and sudden thunderstorms are frequent in July and August. During the winter, temperatures are very cold and snow accumulates to a depth of 8 to 15 feet or more.

During the summer months the trails are used by day hikers, backpackers, and people on horseback. But Mountain Lakes is also a great spot for winter sports. Winter travelers should be aware of the elements and winter survival techniques before entering the Wilderness. Also, please note that the Forest Service cannot mark cross-country ski trails due to Wilderness status.

There are a few rules to adhere to when visiting the Wilderness. First, remember snowmobiles and mountain bikes are not permitted, nor any other type of mechanical item. Because large parties have a severe impact on the environment, groups in excess of ten people and/or pack and saddle animals are not allowed unless a special group permit is issued.

Mountain Lakes is a wonderful place to visit for a few hours, a day, or even a week or more. Relax and enjoy.

For more information contact:

Winema National Forest
Klamath Ranger District
1936 California Ave.
Klamath Falls, OR 97601
(503) 883-6824

Aspen Butte

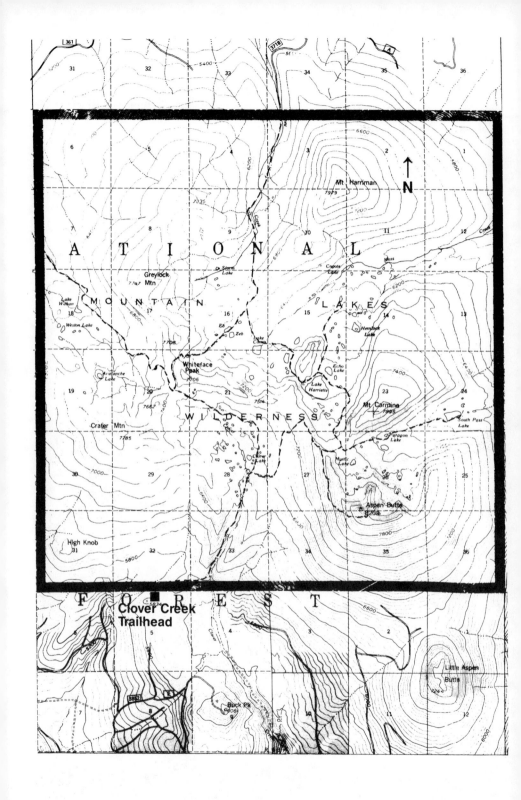

12 MOUNTAIN LAKES LOOP TRAIL

Distance: 13.8 miles
Elevation gain: 2,480 feet; loss: 2,480 feet
High point: 8,208 feet
Usually open: Mid to late June through
late October
Topographic map: Mountain Lakes Wilderness
Obtain map from: Winema National Forest

It's possible to experience the serene and rugged beauty of the Mountain Lakes Wilderness not only in the spring, fall, and summer months, but in the winter months as well. During the summer, the deep blue waters of Lake Harriette invite sweaty backpackers to take a refreshing dip, and in the winter, deep snow lures those on cross-country skis or snowshoes to come and enjoy the peace and serenity.

To reach the Clover Creek Trailhead, drive to the junction of U.S. Hwy. 97, Oregon Hwy. 140 and Oregon Hwy. 66, near Klamath Falls, Oregon. Head southwest on Oregon Hwy. 66 for 9 miles to Keno. Turn right on Clover Creek Road (County Road No. 603) and drive 19 miles to FS Road No. 3852. Head northeast on FS Road No. 3852 for 3.5 miles to a large turnaround and parking area.

Clover Creek Trail No. 3722 begins at the east side of the parking lot. Hike 200 yards or so to the Wilderness boundary then continue the easy hike to Clover Creek at 0.7 mile. Lush ferns hug the sides of Clover Creek and wildflowers abound in the spring and summer months. Look for soft arnica, wandering daisy, monks-hood, arrowhead, butterweed, crimson columbine, and tiger lily to name a few.

The trail curves to the north and heads up the slope following Clover Creek. At 1.9 miles cross the creek and continue the moderate climb up the trail.

At 2.3 miles reach the junction of Clover Creek Trail No. 3722 and the Mountain Lakes Loop Trail No. 3727. Turn right and climb moderately through the forest heading in a north to northeast direction. At 3.6 miles the trail curves and heads to the southeast. At this point the trail is located on top of the old caldera rim. Be sure to walk over to the edge for a wonderful view of Lake Harriette right below the rim and the Klamath Basin to the east.

Continue climbing moderately until you reach the junction of the Mountain Lakes Loop Trail and Aspen Butte at 4.1 miles.

There is an unmaintained trail leading to the top of Aspen Butte. The view from the top of this 8,208 foot butte is outstanding and well worth the climb. Although there isn't room to pitch a tent on top, there is room to throw down a sleeping bag and spend the night. If you need water before you start up Aspen Butte, hike down to Mystic Lake, 0.6 mile away. (Directions to Mystic Lake are included further along in this guide.)

To reach Aspen Butte head south up the trail marked by blazed trees and rock cairns. While it's not the best marked trail, the butte is easy to find. After a 688 foot climb reach the top at 1.2 miles. From this 360 degree vantage point see the Klamath Basin, (including Upper Klamath Lake, the largest natural body of water in Oregon), Mt. Shasta, Mt. McLoughlin, Pelican Butte and more.

Back at the junction of the Mountain Lakes and Aspen Butte Trails, gradually descend by switchback. Head east along the trail as it descends to the junction of the Mountain Lakes Trail and the trail to South Pass Lake at 4.6 miles.

For a relatively uncrowded side trip descend 795 feet on the South Pass Lake Trail to South Pass Lake at 1.6 miles. There are several nice campsites located nearby and the lake is stocked with both brook and rainbow trout for those who desire a scrumptious pan-fried dinner. There are other fish lovers in the Wilderness, too. Look for the bald eagles and osprey that are commonly seen fishing in the area.

If you need water at Mystic Lake head southeast on the South Pass Trail. Just 50 to 75 feet from the junction, South Pass Trail heads to the east. At this point turn off the trail and follow a faint trail 0.2 mile southeast to the lake. Mystic Lake is also stocked with brook trout.

At the Mountain Lakes Trail and South Pass Trail junction, descend moderately via the Mountain Lakes Trail. Pass the rocky slope of Mt. Carmine and at 5.8 miles reach the north shore of

Lake Harriette. The smaller Echo Lake is located just across the trail and down the hill from Lake Harriette's northeast shoreline.

Lake Harriette reaches a depth of 63 feet and is a wonderful lake for swimming. And both Lake Harriette and Echo Lake are fine fishing lakes. Five acre Echo Lake is stocked with brook trout and Lake Harriette is stocked with both brook trout and rainbow trout. There are several nice campsites in the area. Please don't camp near the shore as the shoreline has been completely denuded of vegetation. The Forest Service plans to rehabilitate overused areas such as these in the near future.

To continue on the Loop Trail hike along the trail as it follows the lakeshore then curves away from the north side of the lake at 6.0 miles. The trail climbs a bit then descends a moderate to gradual slope. Continue past a long thin lake on your left and then a series of gradual ups and downs to Lake Como at 7.1 miles.

Lake Como is a scenic lake with Whiteface Peak forming a splendid backdrop. There are many fine spots for camping and fishing here, too. Lake Como is stocked with brook and rainbow trout and there are plans to rehabilitate its lakeshore also.

Descend gradually to the junction of Varney Creek at 7.6 miles. From this point you'll climb gradually to Eb and Zeb Lakes at 8.0 miles. Eb Lake is located on the right and Zeb Lake is on the left. These lakes are small, shallow and not stocked with fish due to winter kill.

After passing these lakes the trail climbs gradually, then at a moderate incline as you begin the switchbacks that lead you to the northside of Whiteface Peak. At 8.8 miles reach a high point with a spectacular view of Mt. McLoughlin, Brown Mountain, and Lake of the Woods.

The trail continues over level ground to the Lake of the Woods junction at 9.4 miles. Stay on the Mountain Lakes Loop Trail and descend gradually to Clover Lake, at 11.3 miles. Reach the junction of the Clover Creek Trail and the Mountain Lakes Trail at 11.5 miles. Continue down Clover Creek to the trailhead at 13.8 miles, thereby completing the loop.

Looking northeast from Aspen Butte

SOUTHERN OREGON WILDERNESS AREAS

Lake Harriette with Mt. Harriman in background

INTRODUCTION TO THE MOUNT THIELSEN WILDERNESS

Mt. Thielsen Wilderness is a combination of mountain peaks and mountain streams, deep blue lakes, a rushing river, wildflowers, wildlife, and majestic beauty.

Hikers making their way up Cottonwood Creek, an area where trails do not exist, find solitude and little evidence of man's existence. And from high atop Mt. Thielsen, they can view the surrounding Wilderness and the mountains and valleys beyond. Throughout, there is beauty for everyone to enjoy.

Located directly north of Crater Lake National Park, Mt. Thielsen Wilderness is situated along the crest of the Cascade mountain range. The nearest town of Chemult, Oregon, 14 miles east, has supplies for those in need.

The Wilderness ranges in elevation from a low of 4,300 feet along the Umpqua River to a high of 9,182 feet atop Mt. Thielsen. Located within the 157,000 acre Oregon Cascade Recreation Area, the 55,100 acre Wilderness contains 78 miles of hiking trails, including 26 miles of the Pacific Crest National Scenic Trail (PCT) which traverses the full length of the Wilderness from a point near Summit Rock to Tolo Mountain.

Three National Forests manage the Mt. Thielsen Wilderness, designated as such by the Oregon Wilderness Act of 1984. The Winema National Forest manages 26,000 acres, the Umpqua National Forest, 22,700 acres, and the Deschutes National Forest, 6,400 acres.

Mt. Thielsen is one of a series of Cascade peaks reminding travelers of Switzerland's Matterhorn. Similar peaks in the Cascade Range include Union Peak, Mt. Washington, and Three Fingered Jack. In his book, *Fire and Ice*, Stephen L. Harris explains why these peaks are so unusual. "Because they all rise from broad, gently sloping bases to extremely steep summits with no trace of a summit crater, these mountains appear unlike any of the other volcanoes in the High Cascades."

Mt. Thielsen, certainly the most prominent peak in the Mt. Thielsen Wilderness, most likely began erupting during the late Pliocene Epoch, producing liquid streams of basalt. During the many thousands of years that followed, these streams combined to form an extensive, gently-sloping shield, not unlike a monstrous inverted satellite television dish.

With a base 11 miles in diameter, and a crater more than a mile and a half across, the shield reached to a height of some 5,000 to 6,000 feet. And because the shield was flat-topped, its slopes reached an angle of only five degrees.

Mt. Thielsen's height was increased to perhaps 10,000 feet as a large pyroclastic cone developed within its summit crater, ultimately filling, then spilling over the brim of the crater and down its sides.

Today, the upper portion of Mt. Thielsen is like a church steeple, its peak a tower standing above the main structure below. The combined forces of erosion and glacier activity stripped away the loose pyroclastic material surrounding the plugs and dikes, exposing what was once the inner mountain.

Mt. Thielsen is often called "the lightning rod of the Cascades." Named about 1872, in honor of Hans Thielsen, a prominent railroad engineer and builder, its spire attracts countless lightning bolts. (For those wishing to climb to the summit of Mt Thielsen, you'll find a trail leading from the southeast side of the mountain to a point near the summit. From this point on some climbers use a safety line, others do not. Your personal preference will determine whether you use some type of gear.)

On the north side of the mountain, hikers will find Thielsen Creek, an excellent place to camp, especially during late summer when the Wilderness is quiet and secluded. The creek bed is a fun place to explore with snow often found along the banks, even in September. And above the creek and the steep talus slopes of Mt. Thielsen clings Oregon's most southerly glacier.

Anglers can cast their lines into Maidu Lake and Lake Lucile, the only lakes located within the Wilderness. Both lakes are usually stocked every two years by the Oregon Department of Fish and Wildlife. Using aerial methods, the ODF&W has introduced populations of eastern brook trout to the once fishless lakes. The North Umpqua River, Evening Creek, and Little Deschutes River support the only other fisheries in the area where small rainbow, brown, and brook trout may be found.

Plant lovers will delight in the array of plants in the alpine, sub-alpine, and coniferous forest zones of the Wilderness. Wildflowers bloom during the late spring and summer months. Flower enthusiasts may find the Cascade daisy, and Suksdorf's campion, both sensitive plants believed to occur in the area.

Wildlife abounds as well, although it is not quite as easy to observe. However, a quiet hiker may a catch glimpse of a deer or elk browsing, or see a black bear ambling up a slope or across a trail. Also, there are many smaller animals in the Wilderness such as pine marten, fisher, badger, fox, and there are even reports of wolverines sighted near the area.

A variety of birds may be viewed while hiking the Mt. Thielsen Wilderness. These include the Clark's nutcracker, common raven, Oregon junco, gray jay, red-tailed hawk, ruffed grouse and blue grouse. In addition, a peregrine falcon has been sighted from the top of Mt. Thielsen, and our national bird, the American bald eagle, has been sighted at Maidu Lake.

Backpackers will want to explore the Wilderness during the summer months when the days are pleasant and the nights are cool. Occasionally a thundershower will roll through the area so be prepared for rain or snow anytime of the year.

As in most high mountain wilderness areas, you're bound to be tormented by mosquitoes just after snow melt. For a more enjoyable visit try hiking the Wilderness in July or later and be sure to bring insect repellant just in case.

Mt. Thielsen Wilderness can be enjoyed in the winter months as well as when a thick blanket of snow covers the land. Nordic skiers and ski mountaineers will find the beauty and peace that only deep snow can provide when visiting the Wilderness during the short, cold days of winter. And to top it off, winter visitors won't be bothered with mosquitoes.

If you'd like the chance to camp at the base of Mt. Thielsen, fish at an emerald blue lake, stand on top of Mt. Thielsen, smell a delicate wildflower, or observe some of God's lovely creatures, visit the Mt. Thielsen Wilderness.

For more information contact:

Umpqua National Forest		Winema National Forest		Deschutes National Forest
P.O. Box 1008	or	P.O. Box 150	or	1645 Highway 20 East
Roseburg, OR 97401		Chemult, OR 97731		Bend, OR 97701
(503) 672-6601		(503) 365-2229		(503) 388-2715

Shelter at Lake Lucile

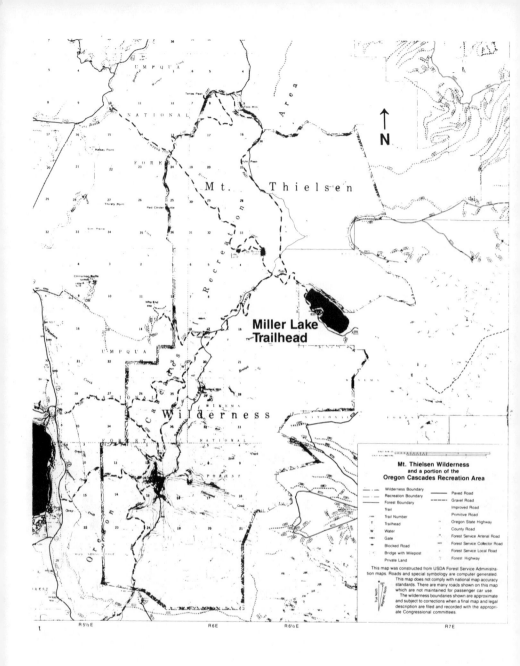

Miller Lake Trailhead

Mt. Thielsen Wilderness
and a portion of the
Oregon Cascades Recreation Area

———	Wilderness Boundary	——— Paved Road
— - —	Recreation Boundary	═══ Gravel Road
———	Forest Boundary	▬▬▬ Improved Road
	Trail	Primitive Road
	Trail Number	Oregon State Highway
T	Trailhead	County Road
W	Water	Forest Service Arterial Road
	Gate	Forest Service Collector Road
	Blocked Road	Forest Service Local Road
	Bridge with Milepost	Forest Highway
	Private Land	

This map was constructed from USDA Forest Service Administration maps. Roads and special symbology are computer generated. This map does not comply with national map accuracy standards. There are many roads shown on this map which are not maintained for passenger car use. The wilderness boundaries shown are approximate and subject to corrections when a final map and legal description are filed and recorded with the appropriate Congressional committees.

SOUTHERN OREGON WILDERNESS AREAS

13 MILLER LAKE to THIELSEN CREEK

Distance: 11.7 miles
Elevation gain: 1,975 feet; loss: 700 feet
High point: 7,550 feet
Usually open: Early July through late
    September
Topographic map: Rogue-Umpqua Divide,
    Boulder Creek and Mt.
    Thielsen Wildernesses Map
Obtain map from: Umpqua National Forest
    Winema National Forest
    Deschutes National Forest

To reach the Miller Lake Trailhead turn left on FS Road No. 9772, located just north of Chemult, Oregon on U.S. Hwy. 97. A sign points the way to Miller Lake – 13 miles east. Follow this road to Miller Lake. At the Digit Campground head to the picnic area where there is ample parking in the day use area. Miller Lake Trail No. 3725A is located near the lakeshore.

Hike the Miller Lake Trail through the trees along the northwest side of the lake. Along this easy trail to the north end of Miller Lake look for downed trees chewed by beaver.

At 0.8 mile reach a sign, "Miller Lake Recreation Area," and a trail heading to the left. Turn left and head up the level trail to 1.1 miles and the Mt. Thielsen Wilderness boundary sign. Cross the bridge at Evening Creek (where the beaver live) and continue up the gradual trail. At 2.7 miles reach the junction of the Miller Lake Trail and the Pacific Crest Trail (PCT). Turn left onto the PCT, heading south towards Crater Lake, twenty miles away.

Climb gradually through a series of slopes and switchbacks before reaching a great viewpoint (rocky outcrop), at 5.0 miles. From this point, looking north, you'll see the shimmering waters of Maidu Lake, and 7,392 foot Cappy Mountain.

The trail now heads southwest and climbs moderately through the forest. Cross a meadow using a fencepost to guide you then continue up the trail. Reach another rock outcrop at 6.3 miles. Now there is a splendid view of the Sawtooth Ridge, Miller Lake, Red Cone, and Cappy Mountain. From the rocky outcrop head southwest and gradually climb then remain level as the trail curves and heads west to Tipsoo Peak. At 6.6 miles the trail curves south.

Gradually climb along the east side of Tipsoo Peak. Tipsoo Peak is a Chinook jargon word for "grass" and also means "hair." The trail climbs through the trees and passes by a large meadow that runs along the east side of the trail.

The trail leaves the trees and climbs through a series of open meadows and small stands of trees. Along this portion of trail there are wonderful views of Tipsoo Peak, the valley towards Chemult and the Sawtooth Ridge. When passing through the meadows follow the posts which are notched or marked with the PCT emblem. At 7.8 miles you're back in the trees and descending moderately to the junction of Homer Spring at 8.0 miles. Homer Spring is located less than one-half mile west on Trail No. 1473.

Begin a gradual descent to 8.4 miles where you'll get a fantastic view—through trees—of Howlock Mountain to the east, and Mt. Thielsen to the south.

The trail curves and descends at a moderate rate to the Howlock Mountain Trail No. 1448 at 8.8 miles. This trail leads to the west and reaches Diamond Lake in 7.0 miles. Another sign points the way to Thielsen Creek located 3.0 miles ahead.

There is a view of Howlock Mountain from this point, then again a hundred yards down the trail. Enter the trees and descend gradually to a small meadow. Follow the posts across the barren area and back into the trees.

The trail is level with some gradual ups and downs as you head to Mt. Thielsen. This section of trail provides wonderful views of Mt. Bailey and Diamond Lake to the west and of Mt. Thielsen off and on through the trees.

At 11.7 miles reach the junction of the Thielsen Creek Trail No. 1449. This trail heads west to some nice campsites and to Diamond Lake, 6.0 miles. Turn right and walk a few hundred yards before reaching some flat sites for camping at 11.8 miles. You can reach the creek from these sites or continue straight ahead on the PCT and cross the creek in another few hundred yards.

While exploring the Thielsen Creek area notice the lava plugs at the head of the creek. For a spectacular view hike up the creek to the saddle at the northeast base of Mt. Thielsen. From this vantage point you'll see Cottonwood Creek to the southeast, Tipsoo Peak to the north and Diamond Peak to the northwest. And don't be surprised to find snow along the creek during the latter part of the summer.

Miller Lake from the Pacific Crest Trail

SOUTHERN OREGON WILDERNESS AREAS

14 MILLER LAKE to TENAS PEAK

Distance: 11.6 miles
Elevation gain: 2,005 feet; loss: 1,150 feet
High point: 6,750 feet
Usually open: Early July through
         late September
Topographic map: Rogue-Umpqua Divide,
         Boulder Creek and Mt.
         Thielsen Wilderness Map
Obtain map from: Umpqua National Forest
         Winema National Forest
         Deschutes National Forest

To reach the Miller Lake Trailhead, turn left on FS Road No. 9772, located just north of Chemult, Oregon on U.S. Hwy. 97. A sign points the way to Miller Lake – 13 miles east. Follow this road to Miller Lake. At the Digit camp-ground head to the picnic area where there is ample room to park in the day use area. The Miller Lake Trailhead is located by a sign near the lakeshore.

Hike the Miller Lake Trail No. 3725A through the trees and along the northwest side of the lake. As you hike the flat trail to the north end of Miller Lake, look for signs of beaver. There are many downed trees in the area, sure proof that beaver may be found.

At 0.8 mile reach a sign, "Miller Lake Recrea-tion Area." Turn left and head up the trail to 1.1 miles and the Mt. Thielsen Wilderness boundary sign. Cross the bridge at Evening Creek (where the beaver live) and continue up the gradual trail. At 2.7 miles reach the junction of the Miller Lake Trail and the Pacific Crest Trail. (PCT).

Turn right at the junction, gradually climb-ing across the slope, and switchback up for a grand view of Miller Lake to the southeast. Gradually climb or remain level to 5.4 miles. Now the trail heads downhill before climbing up a moderate slope. At 6.4 miles cross a shale slope while enjoying the beauty of nearby Cappy Mountain.

Enter the trees, climbing, leveling off, then climbing moderately to a ridge. Continue along the ridge for a wonderful view of the Sawtooth Ridge and Tipsoo Peak. As the trail levels off then gradually heads downhill, look for Mt. Bailey off to the side.

At 7.5 miles there are more views in store as you see Tenas Peak and other peaks to the north-west. Moderately descend through the dense, moss covered trees to Tolo Camp, at 8.5 miles. Tolo Camp is located on a wooded saddle. A few campsites are available with water located on the east side of the ridge via Trail No. 1411. It's an easy switchback of 0.3 mile to a spring that is sometimes quite muddy because folks step in the water. An outdoor toilet is located on the sad-dle though someone tore down the privacy par-tition to use as a windbreak.

Descend and then climb moderately across the slope of Tolo Mountain. Mt. Thielsen and Tipsoo Peak can be seen to the south. Continue climbing then descend or remain level to the junction of the PCT and Tolo Creek Trail No. 1466 at 10.5 miles.

Turn left and gradually descend 350 feet to the junction of Tenas Peak Trail at 11.1 miles. The Tolo Creek Trail continues to Kelsay Valley Trail – 6.5 miles away. Take the Tenas Peak Trail No. 1445 and climb around to the south side of Tenas Peak, then up for a magnificent view that is definitely worth the 330 foot climb. Reach the peak at 11.6 miles.

15 MILLER LAKE to MAIDU LAKE to LAKE LUCILE

Distance: 4.8 miles
Elevation gain: 525 feet; loss: 200 feet
High point: 6,200 feet
Usually open: Early July through late
September
Topographic map: Rogue-Umpqua Divide,
Boulder Creek and
Mt. Thielsen Wildernesses
Map
Obtain map from: Umpqua National Forest
Winema National Forest
Deschutes National Forest

To reach the Miller Lake Trailhead turn left on FS Road No. 9772, just north of Chemult, Oregon off U.S. Hwy. 97. A sign points the way to Miller Lake – 13 miles east. Follow this road to Miller Lake. At the Digit campground head to the picnic area where there is ample parking in the day use area. Miller Lake Trail No. 3725A is marked with a sign and located near the lakeshore.

Hike the Miller Lake Trail No. 3725A through the trees and along the northwest side of the lake. As you hike the easy trail to the north end of the lake, watch for downed trees chewed by beaver.

At 0.8 mile reach a sign, "Miller Lake Recreation Area." Turn left and head up the level trail to the Mt. Thielsen Wilderness boundary sign at 1.1 miles. Cross the bridge at Evening Creek (where the beaver live) and continue up the gradual trail. At 2.7 miles reach the junction of the Miller Lake Trail and the Pacific Crest Trail (PCT).

Continue straight ahead, gradually descending to Maidu Lake. At 3.5 miles reach a sign, "Maidu Lake Trail No. 1446." Bear to the left toward the lake and shelter which needs some repair. The shelter, built by the Boy Scouts in 1961 and 1962, was damaged by a heavy snow load during the winter of 1983-84.

For those that would rather camp elsewhere, there are other campsites along the west and north sides of the lake.

Another good spot for camping, at Lake Lucile, can be reached by passing the Maidu Lake shelter and continuing on around the west side of the lake. Just before reaching Maidu's north shore at 3.8 miles you'll see what appears to be a drainage and a blazed tree. Follow this as it opens into a nice trail with slight ups and downs and level spots to Lake Lucile. If you miss this trail you'll reach a sign saying "Lake Lucile – 1.5 miles and Kelsay Valley Trail – 8¾ miles." This is the long way to Lake Lucile. Backtrack 100 yards and try again to find the blazed trail.

You'll reach the east shore of Lake Lucile in 4.5 miles. Continue around the lake to the southwest side for a nice campsite with another Boy Scout shelter at 4.8 miles.

Camping at the base of Mt. Thielsen

INTRODUCTION TO THE RED BUTTES WILDERNESS

The Red Buttes Wilderness is one of those areas that once visited, just has to be visited time and time again. Something lures a person back. It might be the steep mountain slopes, spectacular viewpoints, colorful meadows, or deep-blue lakes. Maybe it's one of the above, all of the above, or none of the above. Whatever the reason, the Red Buttes Wilderness is definitely worth exploring.

It is located near the crest of the rugged Siskiyou Mountains along the border between southwestern Oregon and northwestern California. Comprised of a chain of peaks, the Siskiyou crest forms the southern boundary of the Wilderness area. These peaks include Red Buttes, Kangaroo Mountain, and Rattlesnake Mountain, all located within the Wilderness.

The Siskiyou Crest serves as a watershed divide between the Rogue River to the north and the Klamath River to the south. A tributary of the popular Rogue River, the Butte Fork Applegate River, begins life as its waters flow out from Azalea Lake, and continue through the heart of the Wilderness. A small portion of the Illinois River drainage is also located in the area.

The Red Buttes Wilderness consists of 20,234 acres ranging in elevation from 3,000 feet along the Butte Fork Applegate River to 6,739 feet on top of Red Buttes.

Three National Forests manage Red Buttes which was designated Wilderness by Congress in 1984. The Rogue River National Forest manages 16,900 acres, the largest portion. In addition, the Siskiyou National Forest manages 3,234 acres, and the Klamath National Forest 100 acres.

There are seven key access points leading to the Wilderness. Also, you'll find the Cook and Green Pass an excellent place to begin a hike into Red Buttes, although it does begin a couple of miles from the Wilderness boundary.

Red Buttes, the 6,739 foot high butte for which the Wilderness is named, and nearby Kangaroo Mountain, are composed of weathered periodotite and serpentine. These reddish-orange mountains, along with other rock types in the vicinity, form inhospitable but scenic terrain which supports a number of unusual plant species.

It is estimated that one quarter of Oregon's rare and endangered plants are found in the Klamath-Siskiyou area. This is due primarily to an intermingling of climates and plant communities where northwest California and southwest Oregon meet.

A dozen or so plants are believed to grow on serpentine rock which is found throughout the area. Plant growth on serpentine soil tends to be sparse, open, and stunted. In addition, some species have adapted specifically to serpentine soil and are rarely found elsewhere.

Steep slopes, some of them rocky and open, others deeply forested with pine, form the rugged terrain. The lower slopes are heavily forested with white fir, Shasta red fir, and Douglas fir. Rocky sites and ridge tops provide open areas although dense brushfields cover many of the steep slopes.

There are some relatively uncommon species of trees to observe when in the Wilderness. Two "weeping" evergreens, the Port Orford cedar and the rare Brewer spruce, are found only in the Klamath-Siskiyou Mountain area. Once widespread, today researchers believe these species are bound to serpentine soils by their inability to compete with other trees where conditions are better. The weeping Brewer spruce is just one of the unique varieties of plant forms and can be seen when hiking near Towhead Lake, along the crest of the Siskiyous near Rattlesnake Mountain, and elsewhere in the Wilderness.

Glaciation has created many interesting geologic features, including several lakes. The lakes found at the highest regions of the Wilderness are carved out basins formed by small glaciers many thousands of years ago. Azalea Lake is surrounded by azalea plants which bloom during the late spring and early summer months. Lonesome Lake, its shoreline also decorated with azaleas, is a scenic lake as well, and both Tannen and East Tannen are carved out lakes situated at the base of 6,298 foot Tannen Mountain.

Meadows are particularly colorful in the spring and summer months. Look for brilliant crimson columbines, their spurred petals similar to an eagle's claw according to some folks. Also, find orange colored tiger lilies, Washington lilies, and giant red paintbrush.

In addition to the many species of plant life, hikers will find an abundance of animal life. Although often hard to observe, there are deer, elk, bear, and porcupine, to name just a few of the mammals found in the area. Also, there are many species of birds including gray jays and Clark's nutcrackers.

Fishing in the Wilderness is quite good. The two small Tannen Lakes have been stocked with fish and there are resident trout within the area. And anadromous fish such as salmon and steelhead can also be found at the lower reaches of Sucker Creek.

This rugged Wilderness is definitely a botanist's paradise. But it's a backpacker's paradise too. There are lakes to swim and fish in, and spots along the trail from which one can gaze at the vast mountains and valleys of two states. And there are meadows to explore, wildflowers galore to see, smell, and remember.

For more information contact the following:

Siskiyou National Forest
Illinois Valley Ranger District
26568 Redwood Highway
Cave Junction, OR 97523
(503) 592-2166

or

Rogue Roger National Forest
Applegate Ranger District
6941 Upper Applegate Rd.
Jacksonville, OR 97530
(503) 899-1812

or

Klamath National Forest
1312 Fairlane Rd.
Yreka, CA 96097
(916) 842-6131

Lonesome Lake

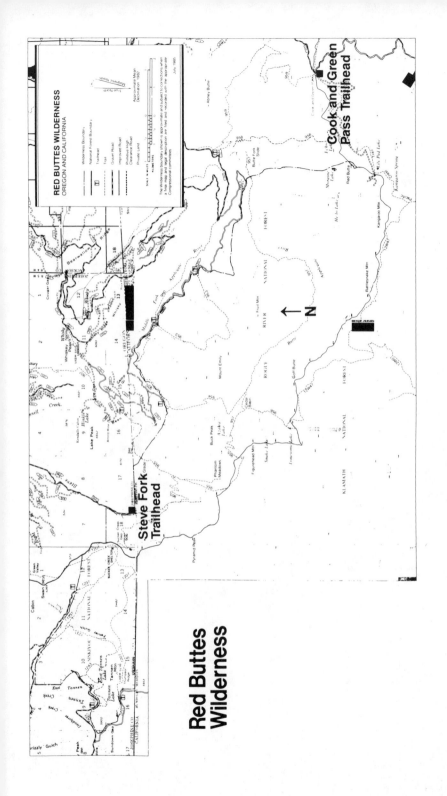

Red Buttes Wilderness

SOUTHERN OREGON WILDERNESS AREAS

16 COOK and GREEN PASS to TOWHEAD LAKE

Distance: 4.5 miles one way
Elevation gain: 1,360 feet; loss: 760 feet
High point: 5,840 feet
Usually open: July through late October
Topographic map: Red Buttes Wilderness Map
Obtain map from: Rogue River National Forest
                       Siskiyou National Forest
                       Klamath National Forest

Towhead Lake is a small, yet scenic lake surrounded by rocky slopes and huge boulders. To the east, Red Buttes looms 6,739 feet, making it the highest peak in the Wilderness. And from the north side of the lake there is a grand view of the surrounding forest with Hello Lake and Hello Canyon visible to the north.

To reach the trailhead at Cook and Green Pass, turn south off Oregon Hwy. 238 at the town of Ruch, located approximately eight miles east of Applegate, Oregon. Head south on Upper Applegate Road towards Applegate Dam. Follow the road as it winds around the west side of the Dam and Applegate Lake. At 20.5 miles from Ruch you'll reach the southwest end of the lake. Turn left on FS Road No. 1050 and follow this past the Applegate River and up the hill, 0.2 mile.

Continue one mile on FS Road No. 1050 then turn right on FS Road No. 1055. At this point you'll see a sign that reads "Cook N Green Pass, 10 miles ahead." Follow this around and up until you reach the junction of the Cook and Green Pass and the Pacific Crest Trail (PCT). There is room to park here, but if you'd rather drive closer to the Wilderness, continue straight ahead along the old mining road 3.6 miles to Lily Pad Lake. This guide begins at the PCT as the road is not maintained and thick brush covers part of it.

This particular hike begins a few miles from the Red Buttes Wilderness boundary. At the Cook and Green Pass/PCT junction, head up the PCT located to the west. For those who need water, you'll find a spring right off Trail No. 959. The spring is located to the right of the trail, just two minutes away.

Climb moderately through the forest then out onto a slope. At 0.8 mile look for Mt. Shasta to the southeast. On a clear day it seems as though you can see forever and even on a hazy day it's possible to see Shasta's huge outline in the distance.

At 1.0 mile the trail heads in a northwest direction with Red Buttes visible across the valley. Gradually climb across the semi-open slope toward Red Buttes. At 2.3 miles come to a fork and a sign leading to Horse Camp Trail No. 958. Just down the hill is Echo Lake and further beyond is Horse Camp.

Gradually descend down the slope and into a forest of ferns and flowers, an abrupt change from the rocky slope you've been climbing.

The PCT crosses the mining road at 2.7 miles. Continue along the trail as it follows the ridge first to the south, then to the west. At 3.6 miles you'll get a glimpse of Lily Pad Lake. Although it first appears to be a dried lake filled with green grass, soon you'll see that it is filled from shore to shore with lily pads.

At 3.7 miles the trail forks and you'll find a trail heading south to Lily Pad Lake. The trail to the right fork heads up to the old mining road. To continue on to Kangaroo Springs or Towhead Lake head straight ahead (west) for a few hundred feet.

If you like great views take the trail to Rattlesnake Mountain. As you hike along the trail you'll see Mt. Shasta to the southeast and Mt. McLoughlin to the northeast. As one hiker put it, "you'll feel as close to being on top of the world as you can for mountains of this size."

While spectacular views are nice, our destination is small, out-of-the-way Towhead Lake. Turn right at 3.7 miles and hike a few hundred feet to the old mining road. A sign points the way down the PCT (the way you just came). This also marks the Wilderness boundary although there isn't a sign stating so. The Forest Service informed me that there was a Wilderness sign and bulletin board on the Wilderness Boundary above Lily Pad Lake, but they were stolen in the fall of 1985.

Head north down the mining road. Some of you may wonder why the road is not closed at the boundary near Lily Pad Lake. The Forest Service informed me that the road is not closed because of mining litigation.

At 4.1 miles you'll reach a fork in the road. Bear to the right and follow it past an old building to the end of the road. A maintained trail isn't available, but there is an old trail leading northwest to Towhead Lake. You'll catch glimpses of it along the way. Bushwhack for the next 0.4 mile as you descend to Towhead Lake at 4.5 miles.

Campsites are limited, although there are a few spots in the grassy area just east of the lake. Please don't camp near the lakeshore. Horses have already muddied up the shoreline. It's difficult to imagine how the horses maneuvered over the boulders and thick vegetation that surround the lake in the first place.

Towhead Lake contains water year-round and is very deep at one end although diving is not recommended. While Towhead Lake may be pretty, it is not stocked with fish, although a skinny one is seen on occasion.

Towhead Lake

Red Butte

Lily Pad Lake from the Pacific Crest Trail

SOUTHERN OREGON WILDERNESS AREAS

17 STEVE FORK TRAILHEAD to LONESOME LAKE

Distance: 9.0 miles
Elevation gain: 1,760 feet; loss: 760 feet
High point: 6,000 feet
Usually open: July through late October
Topographic map: Red Buttes Wilderness Map
Obtain map from: Siskiyou National Forest
                Rogue River National Forest
                Klamath National Forest

Lonesome Lake can be reached by hiking in from several different trails. Starting at the Steve Fork Trailhead offers a nice sidetrip to Phantom Meadows, great views, wildflowers at Azalea Lake, cedar trees in Cedar Basin, as well as lovely Lonesome Lake.

To reach the Steve Fork Trailhead drive Oregon Hwy. 238 to the town of Applegate, Oregon. From Applegate head south on FS Road No. 10 for 15 miles. Turn right on FS Road No. 1030 and continue south / southwest for 11 miles until the road ends at the Steve Fork Trailhead.

Hike around the log barricade and climb gradually up the dirt road and into the Wilderness. At 0.8 mile reach a fork in the trail. Trail No. 906 heads to the right and up to Sucker Creek Gap. (See #18 STEVE FORK TRAILHEAD TO TANNEN LAKE for details.) Stay on the left fork trail as it curves then crosses a couple of dry creeks. Reach Steve Fork Creek at 0.9 mile. Steve Fork Creek is a reliable place to get water as the creek flows all year. Cross the creek and come to the junction of Trail No. 905 and Trail No. 906 at 1.0 mile.

Turn right and climb gradually, heading south to a fork at 1.4 miles. Turn left and begin climbing the moderate switchbacks. As you climb you'll see magnificent Pyramid Peak from vari-

ous points along the switchbacks. At 2.9 miles reach the ridgetop at 5,400 feet for a view of Pyramid Peak to the west, Buck Peak to the southeast, and Fir Glade to the northeast.

Head northeast and begin a series of switchbacks that descend 160 feet and reach the Azalea Lake / Fir Glade Trail junction at 3.2 miles. Turn right on Fir Glade Trail No. 955 and begin the gradual climb towards Azalea Lake.

At 3.5 miles you'll reach the Phantom Meadows junction. The 260 foot drop in elevation and the 0.8 mile hike down the unmaintained trail is well worth the effort. This beautiful little meadow is loaded with numerous species of wildflowers including Kelly's tiger lilies and the giant red paintbrush, among others.

To reach Lonesome Lake, continue the gradual climb to the south while enjoying a superb view of the northeastern section of Red Buttes Wilderness. At 4.5 miles you'll reach the top of the ridge. Notice the view! Fir Glade, Buck Peak and Whiskey Peak are seen when looking to the north, Phantom Meadows is directly below, and to the south you'll see the Marble Mountain Range.

Continue to the south side of the ridge, following the trail as it climbs the open, rocky slope. At 5.5 miles climb a set of short switchbacks to the highest point of the trip at 6,000 feet high. Descend the long switchbacks to Azalea Lake at 6.7 miles.

There are a wide variety of campsites available at various spots around the lake. And for those folks who made a point of bringing their fishing poles, throw in your line. As the sun disappears, ending yet another long summer day, it's easy to see an abundance of fish jumping in the clear blue waters of Azalea Lake. While it is no longer stocked with fish, it is possible to catch some nice German Brown trout here.

Azalea Lake was named for the countless western azalea plants found around its shore. For a special treat visit this area sometime in the spring or early summer when the whitish flowers tinged with pink and yellow bloom.

Nearby you might find another beautiful flower, the Washington lily, also known as the Cascade lily. To observe these lovely flowers you'll have to visit the area in June and July.

To continue on to Lonesome Lake, take the Butte Fork Trail No. 957 to the east. The trail follows the Butte Fork Applegate River which begins at Azalea Lake, and winds through lush, fern-filled forests as you descend to Cedar Basin.

Cedar Basin was named for the many incense-cedar trees which grow here. Also, Cedar Basin consists of wonderful meadows complete with wildflowers in the spring and summer months. In the middle of Cedar Basin, at 7.6 miles, reach the junction of Butte Fork Trail No. 957 and Fort Goff Trail No. 956. (For those that may be interested, the Butte Fork Trail follows the Butte Fork Applegate River to the east side of the Red Buttes Wilderness. Three people were buried near this trail in 1945 when their plane crashed. Parts of the plane remain in the tangled undergrowth along the river, the graves marked by piles of rocks and a headstone.)

To continue on to Lonesome Lake turn right and gradually climb through the forest and into another meadow. Cross the meadow in the middle. Before entering the woods again, there is a ravine to cross. Be sure to cross at the southwest end of the ravine where it isn't quite so deep.

Gradually climb through the woods again then decline gradually and head through another meadow. The trail will curve to the southeast as it follows the edge of the meadow. Shortly after passing a small pond, loaded with lily pads, the trail makes a U-turn as it crosses a stream and heads back along the meadow.

At 8.0 miles you'll climb a couple of switchbacks. At the top of these you'll be able to see Red Buttes and other portions of the southeast section of Red Buttes. Continue along the trail and at 8.6 miles you'll reach a small creek which flows from Lonesome Lake. Cross the creek and take the trail to the right. Gradually climb the trail and at 8.8 miles reach the junction of Fort Goff Trail No. 956 and a trail which leads to Lonesome Lake, but is not marked. If you continue on the Fort Goff Trail you'll head to Red Buttes, but stay on the unmarked trail for a special treat at Lonesome Lake. At 9.0 miles you'll reach the lake. A trail leads you to both sides of the lake.

There are a few nice campsites around Lonesome Lake. Although it was stocked with fish in past years it isn't stocked today and there aren't any reports as to whether or not this is a good fishing lake. Regardless, it's a great spot to swim in or sunbathe next to.

Incense Cedar Tree in the Cedar Basin

SOUTHERN OREGON WILDERNESS AREAS

18 STEVE FORK TRAILHEAD to TANNEN LAKE

Distance: 8.8 miles
Elevation gain: 1,360 feet; loss: 320 feet
High point: 5,440 feet
Usually open: July through late October
Topographic map: Red Buttes Wilderness Map
Obtain map from: Siskiyou National Forest
Rogue River National Forest
Klamath National Forest

Both Tannen and East Tannen Lakes can be easily reached by hiking in from the trailhead near Tannen Lake, located off Forest Service Road No. 4812-041, but hiking in from Steve Fork Road No. 1030 provides a variety of plant and animal life to observe and a chance to view wider vistas.

To reach the Steve Fork Trailhead take Oregon Hwy. No. 238 to the town of Applegate, Oregon. From Applegate head south on FS Road No. 10 for 15 miles. Turn right on FS Road No. 1030 and continue south / southwest for 11 miles until the road ends at the Steve Fork Trailhead.

Hike around the log barricade and begin the gradual climb up the dirt road and into the Wilderness. At 0.8 mile reach a fork in the trail. This fork is not the easiest to see because the trail you're now walking on gently curves to the left and the trail to the right isn't too obvious. Make a sharp right onto the Sucker Creek Gap Trail No. 906. (The trail to the left leads to Lonesome Lake. See #17 STEVE FORK TRAILHEAD TO LONESOME LAKE for details.)

Trail No. 906 heads northwest and climbs moderately through a forest rich in massive Douglas fir, white fir, and occasionally you'll see a Brewer spruce. Look for the long drooping branches, typical of the Brewer spruce. At 1.7 miles cross a creek and continue climbing. The trail curves to the east at 1.9 miles and skirts along the edge of Sucker Creek Gap. At 2.4 miles you'll cross Sucker Creek and follow the trail along the opposite slope. Cross a quaint little meadow then head up the rocky trail to another meadow. Reach Boundary Trail No. 1207 at 2.8 miles. A broken sign marks the junction.

To the right, the Boundary Trail heads northeast through one mile of Wilderness then north to Swan Mountain. There are two trails heading west, the one on the right leads to Sucker Creek Shelter; the one on the left, Boundary Trail No. 1207, leads to our destination, Tannen Lake.

For a nice spot to camp, follow the right trail for a few hundred yards until you see the shelter down the hill and to the right. The three-sided shelter, originally used by cattle riders, was presumably built in the late 1920's or early 1930's, by a rancher named Ashley Fulk.

A trough, filled with spring-fed water, is located nearby. Watch for deer which feed in the flowery meadow and come very close to camp at times.

To continue on to Tannen Lake head back to the junction. Take trail No. 1207 west, climb up the ridge, and hike along the gradual up and down trail. At 3.3 miles reach a sign and junction. Sucker Creek Trail No. 1237 heads north. Continue straight ahead to reach Tannen Lake. Hike through the woods and emerge from the forest onto a ridge at 3.8 miles for a view of Pyramid Peak located to the southeast. Continue along the trail as you hike on both sides of the ridge. Climb the switchbacks at 4.7 miles, then continue 0.1 mile to a point near the top of the ridge. To the north you'll see Swan Mountain.

Continue down the trail for a view of 6,298 foot Tannen Mountain. Follow the trail as it descends gradually and then is fairly level as it reaches the junction of Fehley Gulch and the Boundary Trail at 5.9 miles. Take the right fork, Tannen Lake Trail No. 1243, which leads to Tannen Lake. In a few hundred yards note the sign "Fehley Gulch." This trail heads off to the right in a northeast direction and follows along Thirteenmile Creek.

Continue on Trail No. 1243 to a small stream at 6.2 miles. As you cross the stream and enter the forest you'll wind around Tannen Mountain. In less than a quarter of a mile you'll get a spectacular view of Pyramid Peak to the southeast and all the other surrounding areas. The trail is fairly level as you wind around to Tannen Lake. At 6.6 miles cross a boulder slide and continue to 6.8 miles for a great view to the north. At 7.3 miles the trail turns to the southwest as you make your final approach to East Tannen Lake. Continue through the forest on the level trail and then descend at 7.8 miles.

Tannen Mountain provides a dramatic backdrop for East Tannen Lake. And lily pads, tiger lilies, and a variety of other flowers and plants decorate both the water and shoreline.

Although the lake is no longer stocked with fish, there are plenty of rainbow trout to hook, and a chance of catching some Eastern brook trout, too.

Available campsites are hard to come by in the immediate area. Dense woods and steep hillsides make pitching a tent quite difficult. There are some nice campsites at Tannen Lake though. To reach them continue along the trail, gradually climbing to an open ridge at 8.3 miles. Round a curve and descend to the shimmering waters of Tannen Lake at 8.8 miles.

Fishing for rainbow trout and Eastern brook trout is possible at this scenic lake surrounded by steep mountain slopes. And there are a few nice campsites located around the lake for those who would like to spend a day or two more.

SPECIAL NOTE: While the 8.8 mile hike to Tannen Lake will certainly be worth the effort to some, others might not think so. The scenery from Sucker Gap to Tannen Lake is outstanding, but for those that would like to get to Tannen Lake the easy way, you might be interested to know that you can drive to within 0.3 mile of it. Take FS Road No. 4812-041 to the Tannen Creek Trailhead. Climb a few switchbacks to Tannen Lake.

East Tannen Lake

Sucker Creek shelter at Sucker Creek Gap

INTRODUCTION TO THE ROGUE–UMPQUA DIVIDE WILDERNESS

Flowers sway in the meadows, pine trees reach skyward in thick forests, and fish jump in the clear waters of the many lakes found in the area. And all of this is but a small portion of what each hiker can see and experience in the Rogue–Umpqua Divide Wilderness.

Located in Southwestern Oregon, ten miles northwest of Crater Lake National Park, the Rogue–Umpqua Divide Wilderness rests on the western side of the Cascade Range. As part of the old western Cascade range of mountains, this area developed millions of years ago before the present-day Cascade mountains were formed. As a result, ancient lake beds can be found near Mosquito Lake country in the northeast portion of the Wilderness, and unique rock formations are located throughout many sections of it.

Designated the Rogue–Umpqua Divide Wilderness in 1984 when Congress signed the Oregon Wilderness Bill into effect, the Wilderness was first established as the Rogue–Umpqua Divide Roadless area in 1972. At that time approximately 50,000 acres were set aside for protection. When the 1984 Oregon Wilderness bill was signed, only 33,200 acres of those original acres were designated as Wilderness. However, the remaining 16,800 acres of roadless area will remain unroaded and untouched.

The Wilderness is managed by two National Forests. With 26,350 acres, the Umpqua National Forest manages the largest portion, and the Rogue River National Forest manages 6,850 acres.

From a low of 2,800 feet in the Fish Lake Basin, the Rogue–Umpqua Wilderness reaches to a high of 6,783 feet atop Rattlesnake Mountain. In between, hikers will find timbered valleys and sub-alpine meadows to hike in, and lakes with fish ready for pan-frying. (The Oregon Dept. of Fish and Wildlife uses aerial methods to stock most of the larger lakes with fish.) Some of the trails follow ridgetops where spectacular views of the surrounding mountains and valleys beyond are possible.

There are ten trailheads leading to an extensive trail system that winds throughout the Wilderness. Leading past rock formations such as Elephant Head and the Palisades, the trails provide a variety of scenery for each backpacker to enjoy.

Trails go by meadows where spring visitors can delight in touching, smelling, and photographing a wide variety of brightly colored flowers, some no bigger than a coin, others, like the Washington lily, many times that size.

An assortment of wildlife might also be viewed while hiking the maintained trails of the Rogue–Umpqua. There are elk, deer, mountain lion, black bear, bobcat, and lynx to be found in the area. Of interest to birders are the American bald eagles, as well as the golden eagles and peregrine falcons.

Mosquitoes are a pesky form of animal life in the upper snow fields and around Fish Lake at certain times of the year. For the most part, though, the Wilderness is mosquito free, especially after the month of June has passed, although carrying bug repellant is recommended anytime.

For a bug-free adventure try visiting in the winter months when heavy snow blankets the ground. Nordic skiers will delight in the peace and quiet the secluded area provides. Please note that the Forest Service does not plow the roads leading to the Wilderness.

The Rogue–Umpqua Divide Wilderness is a treat for all who visit whether in spring, summer, fall, or winter. For more information contact:

Umpqua National Forest
Tiller Ranger District
Route 2, Box 1
Tiller, OR 97484
(503) 825-3201

or

Rogue River National Forest
Prospect Ranger District
Prospect, OR 97536
(503) 560-3623

Elephant Head from the ponds near base of Elephant Head

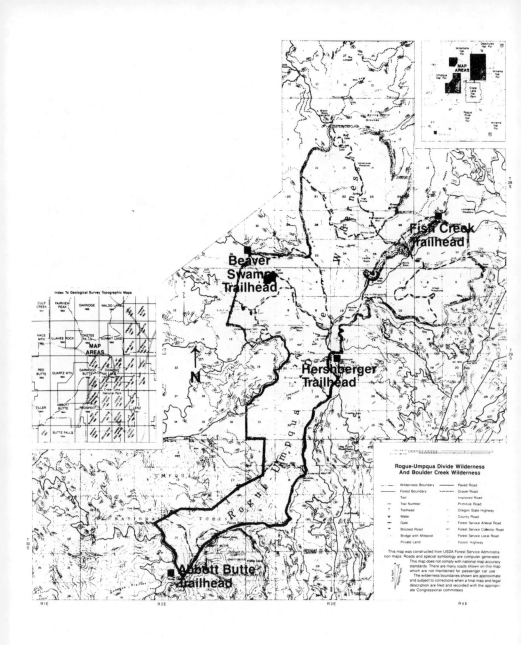

Rogue-Umpqua Divide Wilderness
And Boulder Creek Wilderness

SOUTHERN OREGON WILDERNESS AREAS

19 ABBOTT BUTTE TRAIL-HEAD to ABBOTT BUTTE to ELEPHANT HEAD

Distance: 4.4 miles
Elevation gain: 1,131 feet; loss: 881 feet
High point: 6,131 feet
Usually open: Late June to October–November
Topographic map: Rogue–Umpqua Divide, Boulder Creek and Mt. Thielsen Wildernesses Map
Obtain map from: Umpqua National Forest

This trip is especially nice because the view from atop Abbott Butte is outstanding, because the trail leads through a meadow, and because Elephant Head is a unique rock formation worth viewing up close.

To reach the Abbott Butte Trailhead drive Oregon Hwy. 62 to FS Road No. 68, located four miles south of Union Creek, Oregon. Turn west on FS Road No. 68, continuing past Abbott Creek Campground. At 12.5 miles reach the Rogue–Umpqua Divide at 5,340 feet. Turn right at this point onto FS Road No. 30. Continue to FS Road No. 950, 0.5 mile away. The trailhead is at the end of FS Road No. 950 at 0.2 mile.

The trail begins at the sign "Fish Creek Valley – 22 miles." Descend gradually down Rogue–Umpqua Divide Trail No. 1470. The trail quickly turns into a shaded dirt road then begins a gradual climb to Windy Gap at 0.7 mile. The Wilderness boundary begins in this area although there isn't a sign stating so. From Windy Gap there is a nice view of Crater Lake and Mt. McLoughlin. Head back into the trees and begin a moderate ascent to the junction of the Cougar Butte Trail No. 1432 at 1.5 miles. Continue on past this junction, climbing through an open area, to the junction of Abbott Butte at 2.0 miles.

Abbott Butte is a moderate one-half mile climb to an old fire tower where you'll get a view of the surrounding peaks and valleys. Built in the 1930's by the CCC, the lookout is the second such lookout on the Butte. The lookout was last used on a regular basis in the 1960's, although it was used as an emergency lookout up until the time the area was designated Wilderness. The Tiller Ranger District decided to let the historic structure fall down through natural processes. Today the Butte is a good spot to relax.

To continue on to Elephant Head, hike back down to the junction at 3.0 miles. Descend gradually then level off as you hike through a relatively barren area. A lava field is on the left side of this open area with occasional hemlock, fir and cedar trees. At 3.4 miles reach a sign and trail North / South Trail No. 1433. (Cow Camp – 4 miles, Saddle Camp – 1.5 miles.) The Cow Camp Trail isn't maintained.

Descend gradually through a meadow and an open forest area, crossing a couple of small streams in the process. At 4.4 miles reach two small ponds and a great view of Elephant Head. Beavers built these ponds and keep them there all year.

This area is particularly beautiful in the fall when the colors on the hillside make a spectacular setting for the already amazing Elephant Head.

20 HERSHBERGER MOUNTAIN TRAILHEAD to FISH LAKE to BEAVER SWAMP TRAILHEAD

Distance: 6.2 miles
Elevation gain: 595 feet; loss: 2,195 feet
High point: 6,000 feet
Usually open: Late June to October–November, although Fish Lake Basin is usually accessible most of the winter
Topographic map: Rogue–Umpqua Divide, Boulder Creek and Mt. Thielsen Wildernesses Map
Obtain map from: Umpqua National Forest

The hike from Hershberger Trailhead to Fish Lake is especially beautiful when autumn-colored leaves litter the forest floor. The hike down to Fish Lake is quite a loss in elevation, but well worth it if you'd like to see Hershberger Mountain closeup and for those who crave a bit of exercise. If this doesn't sound exciting, it is possible to reach Fish Lake from the Fish Lake Trailhead and the hike is an easy one, but it is also crowded. Fish Lake is a popular lake and gets a tremendous amount of use. Those desiring solitude would do best to camp in the high country away from the lake.

To reach the Hershberger Trailhead drive Oregon Hwy. 230 to FS Road No. 6510, located 2 miles north of Union Creek. Turn west on FS Road No. 6510, continue 1.6 miles to FS Road No. 6520, then head down FS Road No. 6520 for 0.4 mile. At this point reach FS Road No. 6515 and head left. Take FS Road No. 6515 for 6.8 miles heading past Rabbit Ears, the two rocky peaks to the right. Turn right on FS Road No. 530 to "Hershberger L.O." The trailhead is located 1.6 miles up the road. Just 0.5 mile farther is the Lookout for a view of Mt. Thielsen and other mountains in this area.

The Rogue–Umpqua Divide Trail No. 1470 begins with a moderate climb through the trees for 0.4 mile then descends gradually to the junction of Trails No. 1470 and No. 1570, 1.0 mile from the Trailhead. Take Fish Lake Trail No. 1570 to the left and head toward Fish Lake. (See #22, BEAVER SWAMP TRAILHEAD TO HERSHBERGER MOUNTAIN TRAILHEAD for a return trip via Trail No. 1470 and Trail No. 1572.)

At 1.1 miles you'll see Highrock Meadow and Highrock Mountain through the trees for a spectacular scene framed with fragrant pine trees. Continue descending through the trees then cross Highrock Meadow at 1.2 miles. The trail skirts along the north side of Highrock Meadow before heading back into the trees.

The trail continually descends through the trees at a moderate rate, at times entering areas of deciduous trees. Cross a couple of streams before reaching an area rich in streams, all running into Highrock Creek to your left.

The trail descends down into a steep walled canyon where you'll hike along a shaded side-slope, reaching the junction of Lakes Trail No. 1578 at 3.5 miles. (Trail No. 1578 leads to Buckeye Lake and Cliff Lake.)

Trail No. 1570 remains fairly level until you reach Fish Lake and some nice campsites at 4.1 miles. The fishing is excellent at Fish Lake. Anglers may catch rainbow and German brown trout, both stocked by the Oregon Dept. of Fish and Wildlife using aerial methods.

Hikers will find many fine campsites as they continue hiking around heavily-used Fish Lake. For those planning to return to the Hershberger Trailhead via the same trail, read no further. For those plannning to return via the Rocky Rim Trail, please read on.

At 4.9 miles the trail heads away from the lake and follows Fish Lake Creek for a short distance then heads up at a moderate climb. At 5.2 miles you'll reach the junction of Beaver Swamp Trail No. 1569.

Trail No. 1470 ends at the Fish Lake Trailhead about 4.0 miles away. To reach the Beaver Swamp Trailhead and the Rocky Rim Trail turn right and head up Trail No. 1569. Climb moderately through the trees. At 5.9 miles reach the Wilderness boundary. The trail remains at a gradual to moderate climb and reaches the Beaver Swamp Trailhead at 6.2 miles.

See #22 BEAVER SWAMP TRAILHEAD TO HERSHBERGER MOUNTAIN TRAILHEAD for instructions for the return trip.

Scene near Fish Lake

21 FISH CREEK to ALKALI MEADOWS to HOLE-IN-THE-GROUND to WHITEHORSE MEADOW to THE TOP OF RATTLESNAKE MOUNTAIN

Distance: 22 miles
Elevation gain: 4,006 feet; **loss:** 2,600 feet
High point: 6,656 feet
Usually open: Late June to October–November
Topographic map: Rogue–Umpqua Divide, Boulder Creek and Mt. Thielsen Wildernesses Map
Obtain map from: Umpqua National Forest

This long trip leads through dense forest, open meadows, across streams, and to the top of Rattlesnake Mountain at 6,656 feet.

To reach the Fish Creek Trailhead drive to the junction of Oregon Hwy. 230 and Oregon Hwy. 62, located 1.0 mile north of Union Creek. Here you'll find supplies such as food and gas. Take Oregon Hwy. 230 north for 11.9 miles and turn left on FS Road No. 6560. A sign reading "Buck Creek Canyon" leads the way. FS Road No. 6560 turns into FS Road No. 37 after 4.0 miles. Continue 0.5 mile to FS Road No. 800 and turn left. In 2.7 miles turn left on FS Road No. 870. Take this 1.0 mile to the Rogue–Umpqua Divide Trailhead.

A sign for the Rogue–Umpqua Divide Trail No. 1470 is easy to spot on the left side of the road. Directly across the road from this entrance you'll find the Rogue–Umpqua Divide Trail No. 1470 leading to the Fish Creek shelter. A sign stating so is hidden behind some bushes.

Descend through the trees on a moderate to steep trail and in a few hundred feet reach the Wilderness boundary sign. Continue to the Fish Creek shelter at 0.4 mile. This is a nice spot to camp and there is water available at Fish Creek, located nearby.

The trail is somewhat marked by fence posts and blazed trees as you hike through the trees and meadows of Fish Creek Valley. Sometimes the trail is difficult to follow because of numerous cow paths, but just keep heading southwest and there should be no problem.

At 1.6 miles a freshly blazed trail meets No. 1470. The trail is not signed. If you miss the junction and reach another junction to Windy Gap and Whitehorse Meadow you've gone too far.

Turn left on blazed Trail No. 1477 and head down the trail to the south, across the creek and into the trees. The trail climbs moderately while following a creek. At 2.2 miles rech FS Road No. 870. Cross the road and continue up the moderate slope. You are now hiking on Wiley Camp Trail No. 1046B.

At 2.4 miles the trail begins to descend gradually through a meadow then into the trees where it descends at a moderate angle, sometimes steep. The Wiley Camp Trail is located in a cattle grazing allotment within the Wilderness so be prepared to hike a cattle trodden trail.

The trail levels out some before crossing a creek (no bridge), then arrive at Wiley Camp at 3.1 miles. Wiley Camp is a good spot for camping with plenty of shade and the creek nearby.

Climb gradually to the junction of Buck Canyon Trail No. 1046 at 3.3 miles. Turn right and head to Alkali Lake. (If you miss this turn you'll head straight into FS Road No. 6560 and the Trailhead at Buck Creek.) Follow the trail to Alkali as it gradually climbs and descends through the trees. At 3.7 miles the trail begins to follow a creek. In the fall, autumn colors brighten up this large rocky area where Fish Mountain and Devils Slide dominate the background.

At 4.2 miles cross the creek by stepping on rocks and climb the moderate to steep trail. At 4.8 miles you'll reach a pretty meadow with a spectacular backdrop of Fish Mountain.

Cross the creek near the broken-down bridge and follow the trail across the meadow and into the trees. The trail continues to climb until 5.8 miles when it levels off, then begins a moderate descent to Alkali Meadow at 6.4 miles.

In the spring, hikers will enjoy the many species of wildflowers found in Alkali Meadow. Among the many beauties are Washington lilies and Bog Kalmia.

Continue down the trail until it begins to head southwest. A trail leads to the left and a sign points the way to "Alkali Camp." The camp isn't much to speak of as there aren't many level spots for a tent. It's just an old cow camp, located at 6.7 miles. (There are plenty of good campsites to be found prior to reaching this camp.)

The trail is fairly level as it heads through the trees. At 7.4 miles you'll reach an open area with a good view of Mt. Thielsen. Continue through the trees and cross a creek at 7.6 miles. Climb moderately to an open meadow with a view of Crater Lake National Park to the east, and Rabbit Ears to the southwest. At 8.0 miles you'll reach the junction of the Meadow Creek Trail. Continue across the slope then descend. Notice Hershberger Mountain and Jackass Mountain to the southwest at 8.3 miles. Cross the right side of a meadow. At 8.5 miles cross through a cattle gate then back out onto an open slope.

At 8.8 miles, head back into the trees for a gradual up and down hike. At 9.9 miles begin a gradual downhill and back out into a semi-open area again. At 10.3 miles the trail levels off and then goes up and down. Cross another stream at 10.9 miles and reach Hole-in-the-Ground Camp at 11.0 miles. Hole-in-the-Ground camp is located close to the trail and an open meadow. There isn't any water nearby.

Named because you descend to it, because it is round, and because it sounds hollow when you stomp on the meadow floor, Hole-in-the-Ground is the open meadow you see. If you camp on the meadow listen for deer running across the hollow ground. Jim Hunt, from the Tiller Ranger District, informed me that, "It's like sleeping on top of a drum."

Possibly hollowed out about 100 to 200 years ago, Hunt explained that sulphur from a nearby mine may have caught fire in a lightning storm, burning out a giant hole from beneath the meadow. This is just one theory though, and not a positive answer to the hollowed out meadow.

To continue on to Whitehorse Meadow take the Rogue–Umpqua Divide Trail No. 1470 to the right toward Fish Camp. Those heading left would eventually reach Hershberger Mountain.

The trail climbs at a steep angle across the west slope of Fish Mountain providing good views of Rocky Rim. At 11.7 miles the trail levels off then descends through the trees and reaches a road at 11.9 miles. Descend gradually after turning right on the road. Notice Rattlesnake Mountain, your trip destination, along the way.

At 12.9 miles notice Castle Rock to the west. At 13.0 miles reach the trailhead for Trail No. 1470. Turn left and head towards Whitehorse Meadow. Descend gradually to the junction at 13.7 miles. Turn to the left and head towards Windy Gap, now hiking Trail No. 1477.

Climb the semi-open meadow and at 13.7 miles, cross a creek. Climb and then switchback up and climb moderately around the west side of Rattlesnake Mountain. Reach Windy Gap at 14.6 miles. At the "Windy Gap" sign you'll see the junction of Castle Creek Trail No. 1576 if you look to your left. There is plenty of room to camp at Windy Gap.

Continue up the trail. To the right a trail leads to the top of Rattlesnake. Keep straight as you head to Whitehorse Meadow. The trail follows the tree-covered slope at a level angle and crosses over approximately 16 creeks.

At 15.7 miles the trail continues through huckleberries and rhododendrons. At 16.6 miles you'll see a prominent rocky area to the right. At this point look for a sign "Horse Creek Spring" on the right side. The spring is located across the trail and to your left. The trail begins to head down a gradual, sometimes moderate grade. Reach Whitehorse Meadow at 17.8 miles. Creek water is located just past the campsite as you enter the meadow.

The camp found at Whitehorse Meadow is used by elk hunters during the fall elk season. This camp was complete with fire ring and "hunter's furniture" consisting of four wooden chairs complete with backrests when we were there.

Like Alkali Meadow, Whitehorse Meadow displays a spectacular array of wildflowers in the spring including an abundance of false hellebore.

To reach Rattlesnake Mountain, head back to Windy Gap at 21.0 miles. Head to the left and up Rattlesnake Way (no sign). As you climb the switchbacks notice the grand view of Fish Mountain, Fish Creek Valley, and other areas of the Wilderness. At 21.7 miles the trail begins to descend. To your left is a trail leading to a rock marker on Rattlesnake Mountain. The marker (22.0 miles) is not at the top, but it's an easy climb the rest of the way. (A 360-degree view isn't possible because of dense trees to the north.)

Rattlesnake Mountain was not named for the poisonous reptile its name implies. Rattlesnakes are not found up at this high Cascade elevation, rather the mountain was named for the many switchbacks which lead to its peak at 6,656 feet.

A fire lookout, built in the late teens or 20's, once stood atop Rattlesnake Mountain. The fierce Columbus Day storm of 1962 blew the lookout over. It wasn't in use at that time so efforts were never made to rebuild it.

Alkali Meadow

22 BEAVER SWAMP TRAIL-HEAD to HERSHBERGER MOUNTAIN TRAILHEAD

Distance: 7.5 miles
Elevation gain: 2,560 feet; loss: 900 feet
High point: 6,000 feet
Usually open: Late June to October–November, although Fish Lake Basin is usually accessible most of the winter.
Topographic map: Rogue–Umpqua Divide, Boulder Creek and Mt. Thielsen Wildernesses Map
Obtain map from: Umpqua National Forest

This trail provides grand views of the surrounding Rogue–Umpqua Wilderness, and the valleys and mountains beyond. For those wishing to hike from Beaver Swamp to Hershberger Mountain and back, you may want to return via Fish Lake. (See #20, HERSHBERGER MOUNTAIN TO FISH LAKE TO BEAVER SWAMP TRAILHEAD for details.)

To reach the Beaver Swamp Trailhead from Tiller, Oregon, drive County Road No. 46 northeast to the confluence of Boulder Creek and the South Fork Umpqua River at 14.0 miles. During this stretch of paved road County Road No. 46 turns into FS Road No. 28. Continue on FS Road No. 28 for 10.0 miles to the junction of FS Road No. 2823. Turn right and follow the gravel road for 2.3 miles to FS Road No. 2830. Turn right on FS Road No. 2830 and follow to FS Road No. 2840 another 2.0 miles down the road. Continue 4.0 miles to the large parking area at the trailhead.

From the Beaver Swamp Trailhead parking lot, located on the west side of the Wilderness, begin hiking the Rocky Rim Trail No. 1572, located near the sign which reads: "Rogue–Umpqua Divide – 8 miles."

Begin climbing moderately through the trees, entering the Wilderness at 0.4 mile. At 1.7 miles there is a good view of Fish Lake to the south and Highrock Mountain to the southeast. Just up ahead the trail curves and heads across the front of a rocky area known to some as the Palisades. Next, cross a steep open slope with a great view of Fish Lake and surrounding mountains. Continue into the trees and climb short switchbacks after crossing to the north side of the ridge. At 2.0 miles you'll reach the south side of the ridge for yet another view of Fish Lake.

At 2.3 miles head to the north side of the ridge and up at a moderate climb. At 2.5 miles the trail passes through an open, rocky area then through the trees at 2.9 miles and up the ridge. At 3.2 miles re-enter the Wilderness (the past mile was just out of the Wilderness boundary) then a few hundred feet ahead reach the junction of Trail No. 1571 which heads to the Rocky Ridge Shelter, 2 miles away, and Castle Creek, 4 miles away. (The trail from this point to the shelter is maintained and the shelter is in good condition, although a bit hard to find. The trail from the shelter to Castle Creek has not been maintained for over 20 years now, but will be reopened in 1988.)

Climb a few hundred more yards for a view of the rocky ridge up ahead and Highrock Mountain to the south. A rocky point juts out to the north for those that would like an even better view (including Fish Lake). Also, there is one of several helicopter pads located here. Built before the area was designated Wilderness, the Forest Service is in the process of destroying the existing pads. Such sites would only be used in extreme emergencies now.

The trail continues across the open rocky slope in front of another rocky area, also known as the Palisades, crossing a saddle in a short distance. The saddle is approximately five feet wide and drops off at quite a steep angle on both sides. Now the trail follows along the east side of the ridge providing splendid views of Mt. Bailey, Mt. Thielsen, and Diamond Peak.

The trail continues along an open slope with a level to gradual up and down grade. At 4.2 miles the trail heads back into the trees following first one side of the ridge, then the other, and back to the east side. At 4.9 miles the trail crosses an open slope with good views of Rattlesnake Mountain and Buckneck Mountain. Also, you may notice Hunter Creek mine, a large bare area. In the late 60's and early 70's, miners went into this area and began excavating, looking for gold. When the Forest Service got wind of the situation they stopped the mining pronto. Today the mine is no longer used.

Head back into the trees and gradually climb. At 5.3 miles pass through an open meadow with a view of Highrock Mountain to the southwest. Descend through the trees to another meadow at 5.8 miles. Hike back into the trees and descend to the junction of Trail No. 1470. Turn right on Rogue–Umpqua Divide Trail No. 1470 and hike a gradual up and down grade to the junction of Trail No. 1470 and No. 1570 at 6.5 miles. Turn left on Trail No. 1470 and head to Hershberger Trailhead at 7.5 miles.

INTRODUCTION TO THE SKY LAKES WILDERNESS

The sky reflects its deep blue image into more than two hundred pockets of water at the Sky Lakes Wilderness in southern Oregon. Centuries ago ice fields and glaciers covered this lake-blessed area. Today, hikers won't find ice fields or glaciers, but they will find remnants of the past to explore. There are volcano cores to climb and numerous lakes to fish and swim in. And to make exploring a bit easier there are over 145 miles of maintained trails.

The Sky Lakes Wilderness embraces both the east and west sides of the southern Oregon Cascades. Approximately six miles wide and twenty-seven miles long, the area extends from Crater Lake National Park southward to Hwy. 140.

From a low elevation of 3,800 feet in the canyon of the Middle Fork of the Rogue River, Sky Lakes Wilderness rises to a height of 9,495 feet atop Mt. McLoughlin, the highest point in southern Oregon.

Designated an official Wilderness area in 1984, Sky Lakes consists of 113,413 acres, all of which is managed by two National Forests. The Rogue River National Forest manages the largest portion of the Wilderness with 70,113 acres. The Winema National Forest manages 43,300 acres.

With more than 200 lakes dotting the landscape it is no wonder that they range in size from mere ponds to lakes of 30 or 40 acres. And many of them provide an opportunity for those who enjoy fishing. Please note: Fishing is allowed only with a valid fishing license.

The State of Oregon stocks the heavily-used lakes on an annual basis and some of the more isolated lakes every two or three years. A list of the lakes planted with fish is available from the Oregon Department of Fish and Wildlife.

Huckleberries are a special treat for hungry hikers. Located on both the east and west sides of the Cascades, huckleberries can be found while hiking many of the Sky Lakes Trails, but Wickiup Trail is the best bet for lots of mouthwatering berries.

In addition to an abundance of fish and berries in the Sky Lakes Wilderness there are nearly two dozen tree species to observe and countless species of wildflowers bloom during the late spring and early summer months. In the lowlands hikers will see trees such as the Pacific yew and in the high country there are mountain hemlock and subalpine fir to see and admire. Shasta red fir dominates much of the Wilderness as does lodgepole pine, especially prevalent in the Oregon desert. Flowers and plants consist of the beautiful red columbine flower, kinnikinnick, and huckleberry found throughout the Wilderness.

Wildlife is abundant, also. Roosevelt elk exist in all portions of the Wilderness, especially in the northern sections. On the west side of the Cascades there are black-tailed deer and on the east side hikers will find mule deer. On or near the crest of the Cascades the two species meet and interbreed. Other mammals common to the Wilderness include porcupine, chipmunk, coyote, and black bear. A few years ago, bear were involved in a camp-raiding incidence, but the problem was due to a messy camp. Keep a neat camp and the bears shouldn't present a problem.

Sky Lakes Wilderness can be visited anytime of the year. During the winter months it is possible to cross-country ski over the heavy snow layer which blankets the Cascades. However, backpackers will have to wait until mid-June or even mid-July to visit for the trails aren't snow free until then. At this time of year though, the mosquitoes are fierce and can make hiking into the area quite miserable. The best time to visit Sky Lakes and avoid the mosquitoes would be around August or later.

Little moisture falls from June to October providing for relatively dry excursions. Except for an occasional summer thunderstorm, there is little chance of getting rained on.

The nice weather provides many with an opportunity to climb 9,495-foot Mt. McLoughlin, located in the southern portion of the Wilderness. The six-mile trail to Mt. McLoughlin's summit is not technically difficult, but should only be attempted by persons in good physical condition.

The trail begins with a 4.5 mile climb through dense forest to timberline. Above timberline, for the remaining 1.5 miles, there isn't an actual trail, only circles and crosses painted on boulders. The Forest Service recommends following the same route down as the hiker used to reach the summit.

From the top of the peak each hiker is rewarded for the average four-hour hike with a spectacular panorama of the Sky Lakes Wilderness, and the mountains and valleys beyond. On a clear day it is possible to see south to Mt. Shasta and north to Crater Lake.

Are you in pursuit of a favorite fishing pond? Or maybe you're looking for a belly full of huckleberries? How about finding total relaxation on a day hike to an isolated pond? Would you like to scramble to the top of Mt. McLoughlin? Is a week-long backpacking trip, miles from the trailhead

SOUTHERN OREGON WILDERNESS AREAS

more your style? Are you looking for flowers to touch, to smell, or to photograph? Whatever your plans, Sky Lakes has something for you.

For more information contact the following:

Rogue River National Forest
Butte Falls Ranger Station
P.O. Box 227
Butte Falls, OR 97522
(503) 865-3581

or

Winema National Forest
Klamath Falls Ranger Station
2819 Dahlia
Klamath Falls, OR 97601
(503) 883-6715

Squaw Lake with Mt. McLoughlin in background

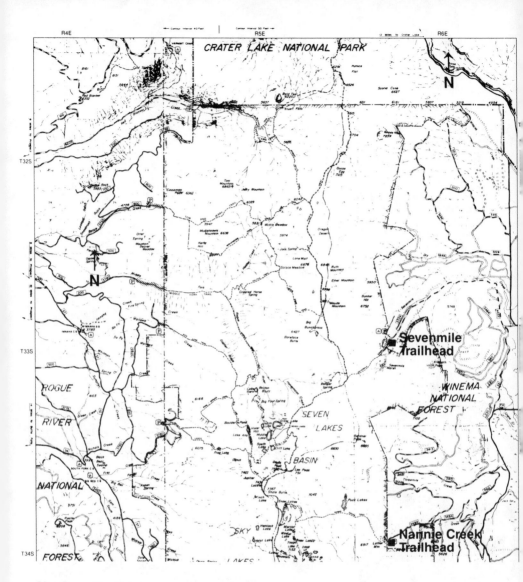

Northern Section

SOUTHERN OREGON WILDERNESS AREAS

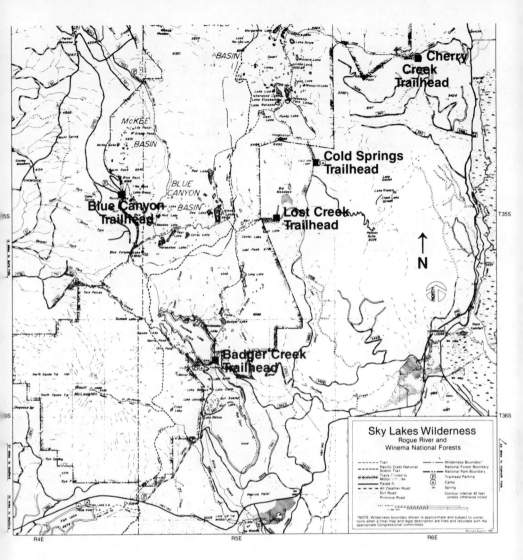

Southern section

23 HEAVENLY TWIN LAKES LOOP TRAIL

Distance: 7.2 miles round trip
Elevation gain: 235 feet; loss: 235 feet
High point: 6,035 feet
Usually open: Late June through October
Topographic map: Sky Lakes Wilderness
Obtain map from: Winema National Forest
Rogue River National
Forest

Clear mountain lakes, and lots of them, are a bonus on this beautiful loop trail located in the southeast portion of Sky Lakes Wilderness. This route passes eight crystalline lakes and an additional four lakes can be found within one-half mile of the trail. No other five mile loop trail in all of Sky Lakes provides access to as many lakes as Heavenly Twin.

The trail begins at the Cold Springs Camp. To reach the camp take Oregon Hwy. 140 to FS Road No. 3651, located approximately 5 miles east of Lake of the Woods. Drive north on FS Road No. 3651 for 10 miles until you reach Cold Springs Camp.

At the north end of the camp you'll find Cold Springs Trail No. 3710. Follow the level trail through the trees to the Wilderness Boundary at 0.5 mile. Continue on, climbing gradually to the junction of the Cold Springs/South Rock Creek trails at 0.7 mile. Bear to the left and continue on the Cold Springs Trail. (This loop will return on the trail to your right, the South Rock Creek Trail.)

Gradually hike along Cold Springs Trail to the junction of the Cold Springs/Sky Lakes trails at 2.4 miles. Turn right onto Sky Lakes Trail No. 3762, reaching the Isherwood Trail junction at 2.7 miles. Now the lake filled loop begins.

Turn left on Isherwood Trail No. 3729, hiking the level trail to two lakes at 2.9 miles. Twenty-seven foot deep Lake Natasha is to your left, three acre Lake Elizabeth is on the right. Both lakes are stocked with brook trout, and rainbow trout can be hooked in Lake Elizabeth, as well.

Continue down the trail to the emerald blue waters of Isherwood Lake and a nice campsite at 3.2 miles. An excellent lake for swimming, there is an area for diving on the west side of the lake. The fishing is also good at Isherwood Lake where it's possible to catch brook or cutthroat trout.

There are a few small unnamed lakes in this area (see map) waiting to be explored. Because Isherwood Lake may be a bit crowded on weekends and holidays those who crave solitude may want to find a campsite near one of these less popular lakes.

Follow the trail around the lake, through the trees, reaching the junction of Isherwood Lake/Sky Lakes trails at 4.2 miles. Turn right onto the Sky Lakes Trail No. 3762. Here you'll find the largest of the Heavenly Twin Lakes – Big Heavenly Twin Lake. The trail heads south on level ground beside both Big and Little Heavenly Twin Lakes. Both are stocked with brook trout. In addition, Big Heavenly Twin contains rainbow and cutthroat trout. If you need water, fill up here, but be sure to boil it before drinking. This is the last opportunity for water before reaching the trailhead.

Between Big and Little Heavenly Twin Lakes you'll come to the South Rock Creek Trail No. 3709 at 4.7 miles. Follow this trail as it descends gradually to the trailhead at 7.2 miles.

SOUTHERN OREGON WILDERNESS AREAS

24 COLD SPRINGS TRAILHEAD to DEVILS PEAK LOOP

Distance: 25.5 mile loop
Elevation gain: 1,560 feet; loss: 1,460 feet
High point: 7,300 feet
Usually open: Late June through October
Topographic map: Sky Lakes Wilderness
Obtain map from: Winema National Forest
                                Rogue River National
                                Forest

After a long hike through the trees, this loop trail provides excellent views of the Southern Cascades. From a point near Luther Mountain, where the trail leads across open shale slopes, it is possible to see for miles when looking to the east, north, and south. And as the trail heads on over to Devils Peak, each hiker will be rewarded with wonderful views of the Sky Lakes Wilderness and beyond.

To reach the Cold Springs Trailhead drive Oregon Hwy. 140 to FS Road No. 3651, located approximately 5 miles east of Lake of the Woods. Take FS Road No. 3651 north until it ends at the trailhead, 10 miles away.

Begin hiking the Cold Springs Trail No. 3710, gradually climbing through the forest to the Wilderness boundary at 0.5 mile. Continue up the trail to a fork at 0.7 mile. Take the left fork and continue up the Cold Springs Trail. (South Rock Creek Trail, the trail to the right, will provide our return on this long, loop trail.)

Gradually climb then descend to the junction of the Cold Springs/Sky Lakes trails at 2.4 miles. Take the Sky Lakes Trail No. 3762 to your left and continue to Deer Lake at 2.8 miles. Stocked with brook trout, this five acre lake is a nice spot for lunch.

Continue on the trail as it climbs and crosses a slope. Reach the junction of the Sky Lakes/Pacific Crest Trail (PCT) at 3.8 miles. Devils Peak is now 7.5 miles to the north. Head north (right) on the PCT and gradually climb through the forest and an occasional meadow for the next couple of miles. Purple lupine flowers cover the ground as you walk through parts of this area in early summer.

At 5.6 miles the trail curves south then heads north again and follows an open slope. Here you'll receive a great view of Oregon's largest natural lake, Upper Klamath. At 5.9 miles cross over to the west side of the ridge and descend by switchback. Follow the trail as it winds through forest and meadow, traveling first on one side of the ridge, then on the other.

At 6.5 miles reach the Cascade Summit at 6,585 feet and Trail No. 986 to Wickiup Meadows, four miles away and to the west. Also, you'll find a trail leading east to Land Lake. (Please note: The Forest Service has abandoned both trails.) Also the Cascade Summit does *not* mark Oregon's high point on the PCT.

Soon after reaching this junction you'll climb to the east side of the ridge for a view of four prominent peaks. Look for Cherry Peak to the east, Lather Mountain to the northeast, Mt. McLoughlin to the south, and Pelican Butte to the southeast. Continue across the rocky slope then gradually climb along the mostly exposed slope to the junction of the Divide Trail and the PCT at 8.5 miles.

The Divide Trail leads to the clear waters of Margurette and Trappers Lakes. These will be visited on our return loop so continue north to Devils Peak. As you hike along the trail towards Devils Peak you'll see Tsugo Lake located at the base of Luther Mountain. Follow the trail as it crosses over a ridge, first through the trees then out onto a boulder field. To the west you'll see Rustler Peak with a lookout station perched on top of the mountain.

At 9.3 miles you'll reach the junction of the Snow Lakes Trail and the PCT. If the mosquitoes are bad you might want to camp on the flat ridge located near this junction. If a breeze is blowing you'll find some relief here. Climb gradually past the junction and enter the forest. Follow the trail over shale rock. At 10.0 miles you'll hike onto an open rock slope for a good view of Mt. McLoughlin, which dwarfs the closer summit of Luther Mountain.

Continue up Shale Butte to the top of a ridge for a nearly 360 degree view of the surrounding countryside. To the southwest you'll see Hemlock Lake and Hoist Lake. Climb moderately up the slope as it winds around the west side of Shale Butte. At 10.8 miles reach a sign for Finch Lake, named in memory of Douglas B. Finch, a fire control officer for the Rogue River National Forest. The lake is located below and to the southwest of the marker.

Continue across the east slope of Lucifer Mountain, reaching the junction of the Seven Lakes Trail and the PCT at 11.2 miles. Continue along the trail as it gradually climbs to Devils Peak at 11.9 miles. At this point – the saddle between Devils Peak and Lee Peak – the PCT reaches 7,300 feet, the highest point on the PCT in Oregon. This is an excellent spot for a rest or picnic and a fantastic view of 7,582 foot Devils Peak. Near the summit a trail heads to the left and up Devils Peak. Follow this for an easy seven-minute climb to the top for a 360 degree view of the surrounding mountain peaks and valleys.

To return to our original starting point at the Cold Springs Trailhead, head back to the junction of the Snow Lakes Trail and the PCT at 14.5 miles. Turn left on the Snow Lakes Trail No. 3739 and descend the shale slope to an unnamed lake on the right at 14.7 miles. Continue along the trail to another unnamed lake on the left at 14.8 miles.

Follow the trail as it heads north along another shale slope. At 15.2 miles the trail heads east and descends to a variety of lakes, some clear and blue, some cloudy. Begin a series of switchbacks after passing these lakes and descend to another of the Snow Lakes chain. Follow the trail as it descends gradually through the trees and then heads south. At 16.9 miles reach the Nannie Creek and Puck Lakes junction. Continue straight ahead on the Snow Lakes Trail to complete the loop. Follow the trail along the drainage to Martin Lake at 17.5 miles.

To Reach Snow Lake (which appears to harbor less mosquitos than Martin Lake) continue south to 17.7 miles. Luther Mountain looms in the background of this gorgeous lake. On the southwest side of Snow Lake there is a boulder field and a nice little drainage complete with wildflowers. This is a good spot for swimming as it is deep and very refreshing. Also, anglers will want to try and hook a brook trout in this small, three-acre lake.

At 18.4 miles reach the Donna Lake Loop Trail. This flat trail leads to three small, but pretty lakes and the trail meets with the Sky Lakes Trail near Trappers Lake, at 0.8 mile. To continue along the Snow Lakes Trail head south until you reach Margurette Lake at 18.7 miles.

Margurette Lake is in the process of restoration on the southwest shore. "Restoration Site – Please No Camping" signs are located in several sites throughout the area. Please give the native vegetation a chance to grow and camp elsewhere.

To reach another beautiful lake head east along the trail and at 18.9 miles reach the north end of Trappers Lake. Both Trappers and Margurette Lakes are stocked with brook trout and Margurette also has rainbow trout in its waters. There are some nice campsites on a few of the bluffs above the lake. Also, this is the entrance to the Donna Lake Trail.

Follw the Sky Lakes Trail No. 3762 around the east side of Trappers Lake. At 19.0 miles you'll reach the Cherry Creek Trail junction to the left. The trail gradually climbs and descends as you continue heading south along Trappers Lake. At 19.4 miles pass Lake Sonya on your left. Reach the Sky Lakes Trail/Isherwood Trail junction at 21.0 miles. Here is one of two Heavenly Twin Lakes. Continue straight ahead if you'd like to visit these two lakes. Turn right to continue the loop.

Isherwood Lake Trail No. 3729 leads over fairly level terrain to Isherwood Lake at 21.7 miles. Continue 0.3 mile to a nice campsite where you can fish for brook trout, swim, and relax.

Hike past Isherwood Lake and at 22.2 miles pass Lake Elizabeth on your left. A short distance ahead and Lake Natasha looms big and blue on your right. Again, both lakes are stocked with trout. Reach another Isherwood Trail/Sky Lakes junction at 22.5 miles. Turn left onto Sky Lakes Trail No. 3762 and descend gradually to the smallest of the Heavenly Twin Lakes at 22.8 miles. There is another restoration site here so please, "No Camping."

At 23.0 miles reach the Sky Lakes Trail/South Rock Creek Trail junction. Turn right (south) on South Rock Creek Trail No. 3709 and gradually descend to the junction of South Rock Creek and Cold Springs trails at 24.7 miles. Head to the left and continue to the trailhead at 25.5 miles.

Pacific Crest Trail south of Devils Peak

SOUTHERN OREGON WILDERNESS AREAS

25 LOST CREEK TRAILHEAD to RED LAKE and ISLAND LAKE LOOP

Distance: 9.1 miles
Elevation gain: 380 feet; loss: 380 feet
High point: 6,000 feet
Usually open: Late June through October
Topographic map: Sky Lakes Wilderness Map
Obtain map from: Winema National Forest
                                Rogue River National Forest

Visiting both Island and Red Lakes is easy via the Lost Creek Trailhead. While the lakes are scenic, they can also be quite crowded, especially during the weekends and holidays. There is a short, direct route to Island Lake, however we've extended the trip by hiking the PCT and making it a loop trail.

To reach the Lost Creek Trailhead drive Oregon Hwy. 140 to FS Road No. 3651, located approximately five miles east of Lake of the Woods. Head north and reach a junction at 8.5 miles. Turn left on FS Road No. 3659 and drive 1.3 miles to the Lost Creek Trailhead.

Begin hiking on Lost Creek Trail No. 3712, a easy hike through the forest, reaching the Wilderness boundary at 0.5 mile. At 1.4 miles you'll see a large meadow (Center Lake) on the left. At 1.5 miles reach the junction of the Badger Lake/Lost Creek trails. A short distance farther reach the Pacific Crest Trail (PCT). Turn right on the PCT and follow the level trail to the junction of Red Lake/PCT trails at 4.3 miles.

Head southwest on the Red Lake Trail No. 987 and hike this easy trail, reaching Red Lake at 5.5 miles. There are a few campsites around this pretty, 29 acre lake. Those who like to fish might hook a brook trout or two.

Continue on Red Lake Trail, passing three small lakes, each about one-quarter mile apart. At 6.7 miles you'll see Island Lake to your right. There are a few nice campsites at this end of the lake with additional campsites at the south end of the lake. Island Lake is also stocked with brook trout.

To camp at the south end of Island Lake, hike to the junction of Red Lake/Blue Canyon trails at 7.1 miles. Head west on the Blue Canyon Trail No. 982 for 0.3 mile where you'll find some nice campsites. Those visiting this area will undoubtedly see the Judge Waldo tree, a Shasta red fir that has been fenced to protect and identify the site. The tree was named for Judge Waldo, who in 1888, along with several others, surveyed the area. Judge Waldo was responsible for instigating the Cascade Reserve. The survey party carved their names in the tree in 1888.

To complete the loop, backtrack to the Lost Creek/Badger Creek Trail junction. Head east and reach the trailhead at 9.1 miles.

26 HORSESHOE LAKE LOOP

Distance: 6.1 miles
Elevation gain: 460 feet; loss: 460 feet
High point: 6,200 feet
Usually open: Late June through October
Topographic map: Sky Lakes Wilderness
Obtain map from: Winema National Forest
                 Rogue River National Forest

This loop begins with a hike down a little used trail that not only provides solitude, but also a spectacular view of nearby Mt. McLoughlin. And on the return loop there is a visit to Horseshoe Lake.

To reach the Blue Canyon Trailhead drive to the junction of FS Road No. 30 and FS Road No. 34, located just east of Butte Falls, Oregon. Head north then east on FS Road No. 34 for 2 miles. At this point turn right onto FS Road No. 32, driving for another 15 miles. Again turn right and take FS Road No. 3770 for 6.5 miles to the trailhead.

From the ample Blue Canyon parking lot walk through the wooden gate and follow the sign that points the way south to Cat Hill Way Trail No. 992. Follow the easy, yet uncrowded trail through the trees, and at 0.5 mile enjoy the view of Mt. McLoughlin. It's an easy hike from here to the junction of Meadow Lake / Cat Hill Way trails at 2.0 miles.

Turn left at the junction onto Meadow Lake Trail No. 976 and descend moderately then gradually to the Meadow Lake / Blue Canyon Trail junction at 3.2 miles. Turn right on Blue Canyon Trail No. 982 and continue the easy hike to Horseshoe Lake at 3.5 miles.

Much of the area has been reforested so campsites are limited, but there are a few nice spots for camping at the west end of the lake. A sign "Camping" points the way to a secluded spot where you might have a few deer visiting your camp. In addition, twenty-acre Horseshoe Lake has been stocked with both brook and rainbow trout.

Before completing the loop and heading back to the trailhead some hikers may want to visit Pear Lake located 0.5 mile to the east. Also, Island Lake is located 2.3 miles to the east. (See #25 LOST CREEK TRAILHEAD TO RED LAKE AND ISLAND LAKE for more details.)

To complete the loop head back to the Meadow Lake / Blue Canyon Trail junction at 3.8 miles. Turn right on the Blue Canyon Trail hiking across level ground to Blue Lake at 4.2 miles. Blue Lake is also a heavily used area with reforestation efforts in progress. Please use designated "Camping" sites.

Now the trail gradually climbs to Round Lake at 5.2 miles. Anglers may hook a brook trout at both Blue and Round Lakes. From Round Lake climb moderately for a short distance before leveling off and reaching the trailhead at 6.1 miles.

SOUTHERN OREGON WILDERNESS AREAS

27 BLUE CANYON TRAILHEAD to SQUAW LAKE

Distance: 5.4 miles
Elevation gain: 280 feet; loss: 915 feet
High point: 6,540 feet
Usually open: Late June through October
Topographic map: Sky Lakes Wilderness
Obtain map from: Winema National Forest
Rogue River National Forest

hike to the junction of Meadow Lake / Cat Hill Way trails at 2.0 miles.

Continue south on Cat Hill Way, climbing moderately. At 2.2 miles look to the north and see the top of Blue Rock. Climb gradually then slowly descend for a view of Mt. McLoughlin's north side. Descend moderately to the PCT / Cat Hill Way jct. at 3.3 miles.

Turn right, heading south on the PCT toward Hwy. 140 (9 miles away). As you descend gradually there are several points that provide a nice view of Fourmile and Squaw Lake. Reach the junction of the Twin Ponds / PCT trails at 4.9 miles. (Twin Ponds Trail follows the path of the Rancheria Trail, an old Indian travel route. Widened in 1863, the path was used as a military wagon road extending between Jacksonville and Fort Klamath. Today this portion of the Rancheria Trail is listed on the National Register of Historic Places.)

At the junction, turn left onto Twin Ponds Trail No. 3715, heading southeast along the level trail. Reach Squaw Lake in 5.4 miles. There are excellent campsites located off the trail that circles the lake. Most of the campsites on the east side of Squaw Lake provide a view of Mt. McLoughlin. It's even possible to see hikers at the top of the mountain. And for a short trip to Fourmile Lake, head east through the trees.

The fishing is excellent at both Fourmile Lake and Squaw Lake where hikers may catch brook trout and at Fourmile Lake maybe a kokanee.

Hikers who live for wonderful views will enjoy this hike even though there are shorter routes to Squaw Lake. Along this hike you'll see the magnificent north side of Mt. McLoughlin looming 9,495 feet in the not-so-far distance. Farther along, as the trail descends, hikers will have a view of Fourmile and Squaw Lakes.

To reach the Blue Canyon Trailhead drive to the junction of FS Road No. 34 and FS Road No. 30, located a short distance east of Butte Falls. Head north then east on FS Road No. 34 for 2 miles. Next, turn right on FS Road No. 32 and drive for 15 miles. Again, turn right on FS Road No. 3770, driving 6.5 miles to the trailhead.

Park in the ample parking area, head through the wooden gate and turn south on the first trail, Cat Hill Way Trail No. 992. Follow the easy, uncrowded trail through the trees to 0.5 mile for a view of Mt. McLoughlin. Continue the easy

Cliff Lake — Devils Peak in background

Reforestation site at Margurette Lake

28 FOURMILE LAKE to BLUE CANYON TRAIL LOOP

Distance: 15.1 miles
Elevation gain: 1,150 feet; loss: 1,150 feet
High point: 6,540 feet
Usually open: Late June through October
Topographic map: Sky Lakes Wilderness
Obtain map from: Winema National Forest
Rogue River National Forest

This loop passes by plenty of lakes good for fishing and swimming. Fourmile Lake, starting point for the loop, is especially popular with anglers who catch brook trout and kokanee in the 740 acre lake.

To reach the trailhead drive Oregon Hwy. 140 to FS Road No. 3661, located near the turnoff for Lake of the Woods. Head north on No. 3661 until the road ends at Fourmile Campground, nearly six miles from Hwy. 140. The campground has fire pits, picnic tables and outhouses. Turn right at the campground and continue to the Badger Creek Trailhead parking area.

Begin a gradual climb north through the trees on Badger Lake Trail No. 3759, entering the Wilderness at 0.3 miles and reaching Woodpecker Lake at 1.2 miles. Along the way there are some nice views of Fourmile Lake with Mt. McLoughlin in the background. As you pass Woodpecker Lake, climb a short hill then descend slowly to Badger Lake at 1.5 miles. Both of these small lakes are stocked with brook trout.

As you hike around the east shore of Badger Lake cross a small stream and continue gradually uphill. At 2.0 miles reach a meadow on the right. The trail follows alongside sections of meadow for about 0.5 mile. Climb gradually to Long Lake at 3.0 miles. The trail passes by Long Lake, revealing a couple of campsites located on the west side of the lake. Again, anglers may catch brook trout in this lake.

The trail heads away from Long Lake at 3.5 miles. Continue an easy hike with a very gradual climb to the junction of the Badger Lake/Lost Creek trails at 4.7 miles.

Turn left on Red Lake Trail No. 987, crossing

the PCT in a short distance. Continue on to the Red Lake/Blue Canyon Trail junction at 5.1 miles. Head west on Blue Canyon Trail No. 982, reaching trout-filled Island Lake at 5.4 miles.

There are a few campsites in the area, but much of the area is in the process of being reforested. Please make note of those areas and camp elsewhere. There are also a few good campsites on the north end of the lake. To reach this area hike back to Red Lake Trail then head north for less than one-half mile.

At the south end of the Island Lake hikers will find the Judge Waldo Tree. Fenced to protect and identify the site, this Shasta red fir was named for Judge Waldo, who in 1888, along with several others, surveyed the area. Judge Waldo was responsible for instigating the Cascade Reserve. The survey party carved their names in the tree in 1888.

To continue on, hike the Blue Canyon Trail, heading west. The trail very gradually climbs and descends, passing a creek at 6.5 miles. At 7.2 miles there is a trail leading to Pear Lake on your left. This 25 acre lake has been stocked with rainbow trout and brook trout. Pear Lake has also been over-used, resulting in more "reforestation" signs.

From Pear Lake hike to Horseshoe Lake at 7.7 miles. Horseshoe Lake is also stocked with rainbow and brook trout. There is a secluded designated campsite on the west end of the lake with a flat, grassy site for a tent. A sign "camping" points the way.

To continue the loop, hike Blue Canyon Trail to the Blue Canyon/Meadow Lake Trail junction at 8.0 miles. Turn left, gradually climbing southwest on Meadow Lake Trail No. 976. The trail climbs moderately before reaching the Cat Hill Way Trail at 9.2 miles.

Head south on Cat Hill Way Trail No. 992, climbing moderately then descending at a gradual to moderate rate before reaching the PCT at 10.5 miles. Along this portion of trail there are some great views of Mt. McLoughlin's north side.

Turn right on the PCT and head south towards Hwy. 140, located 9 miles away. As you descend gradually you'll see Fourmile Lake and Squaw Lake off to the southeast. At 12.1 miles reach the PCT/Twin Ponds Trail junction. (The Twin Ponds Trail follows the path of the old Rancheria Trail, an Indian travel route. Widened in 1863, the path became a military wagon road that extended from Jacksonville to Fort Klamath. Today this portion of the Rancheria Trail is located on the National Register of Historic Places).

Stuart Falls

Make a left on Twin Ponds Trail No. 3715 and hike the level trail to Squaw Lake at 12.6 miles. There are brook trout in this 26 acre lake and campsites on both sides of it. And hikers making camp on the east side of the lake will have a nice view of Mt. McLoughlin.

To end the loop, continue past Squaw Lake, hiking through an area of lodgepole pine to the Wilderness boundary at 13.9 miles. At 14.4 miles reach Fourmile Lake and the campground. Hike along the south end of the lake to the trailhead at 15.1 miles.

29 SEVENMILE TRAILHEAD to STUART FALLS

Distance: 11.7 miles
Elevation gain: 1,080 feet; **loss:** 1,180 feet
High point: 6,680 feet
Usually open: Late June through October
Topographic map: Sky Lakes Wilderness
Obtain map from: Winema National Forest
Rogue River National Forest

the Sky Lakes Wilderness. Bordering on the south end of Crater Lake National Park, the falls provide an ideal spot for spending a day or two.

To reach the Sevenmile Trailhead travel 4 miles west on Nicholson Road from the small town of Fort Klamath, Oregon. Turn left on FS Road No. 3300 for 0.2 mile then turn right on FS Road No. 3334. Follow No. 3334 until it ends at the trailhead, 6 miles from Nicholson Road.

From the trailhead, hike Sevenmile Trail No. 3703 to the Wilderness boundary just 100 yards from the parking area. Continue the easy climb through the trees to the junction of the PCT/Sevenmile trails at 1.8 miles. Turn right onto the PCT and head toward Crater Lake, 10.5 miles away.

It's an easy hike to a trail leading to Ranger Spring, located 1.0 mile to the west. Most folks think the first creek they come to is Ranger Spring. It isn't. Continue through the meadow and follow the trail as it curves through the trees to Ranger Spring where the trail ends. Spring water bubbles and flows in large quantities year-round at this scenic spring.

Back on the PCT, gradually climb to the junction of the McKie Camp and the PCT at 4.1 miles. Continue north along the west side of Maude Mountain. Bunker Hill can be seen to the east of Maude.

At 6.3 miles reach the turn-off for Jack Spring. (This spring is just 0.5 mile to the west.) Continue through the flat Oregon Desert where sparse lodgepoles grow in twisted, bizarre shapes. At 7.9 miles reach the junction of the PCT and the Stuart Falls trails.

Head northwest on the Stuart Falls Trail No. 1078. At 8.1 miles reach another trail heading to McKie Camp Trail. Continue on Stuart Falls Trail while slowly descending through the trees. Huckleberries abound along the trail before the junction of Lucky Camp Trail at 10.5 miles. At 11.4 miles reach the junction of the Upper Red Blanket Trail.

Reach Stuart Falls at 11.7 miles. A sign points the way to the cascading waters. In addition to the beauty of the falls, there are delicate wildflowers during the early summer months bordering the ice-cold creek water.

Camping is not allowed near the falls due to another attempt at reforestation. But there are a couple of handy campsites located away from the falls where the sound of rushing water can still be heard. Also, there are huge piles of cut firewood. The Forest Service cut down some snags in the area, then cut the snags into firewood, and hope to burn it someday soon so you may or may not find the firewood there.

This trip is particularly fascinating because it leads through the flat, dry Oregon Desert and on up to Stuart Falls, the northernmost point in

30 OREGON DESERT – ROGUE RIVER – SEVEN LAKES BASIN LOOP

Distance: 27.9 miles
Elevation gain: 3,850 feet; 4,050 feet
High point: 6,600 feet
Usually open: June through October
Topographic map: Sky Lakes Wilderness
Obtain map from: Winema National Forest
                    Rogue River National Forest

This long loop trail will thrill those hikers who love variety. The trail passes across the flat Oregon Desert, through lush meadows, then down to the Rogue River. And from there the trail steepens dramatically while climbing through fern-covered forest to the Seven Lakes Basin.

The loop begins at the Sevenmile Trailhead. To reach the trailhead travel four miles west on Nicholson Road from the quaint little town of Fort Klamath, Oregon. Turn left on FS Road No. 3300, traveling 0.2 miles before turning right on FS Road No. 3334. Follow No. 3334 until it ends at the trailhead, 6 miles from Nicholson Road.

From the trailhead hike Sevenmile Trail No. 3703 through the trees to the Wilderness boundary just 100 yards from the parking area. Continue the easy climb to the junction of the Sevenmile Trail/Pacific Crest Trail (PCT) at 1.8 miles. Turn right on the PCT and head toward Crater Lake, 10.5 miles away.

At 2.0 miles reach a trail heading west to Ranger Spring. Ranger Spring provides a bountiful supply of water which spills out onto the meadow nearby. To reach the spring follow this trail 1.0 mile. The trail passes through a meadow and into the trees where the trail ends and the spring begins.

To continue the loop, gradually climb north on the PCT reaching the junction of McKie Camp/PCT trails at 4.1 miles. Continue north along the west side of Maude Mountain. Bunker Hill can be seen to the east of Maude Mtn.

At 6.3 miles reach a trail leading to Jack Spring, located 0.5 miles to the west. Next enter the Oregon desert, hiking the flat trail as it leads past twisted lodgepole pines. At 7.9 reach the junction Stuart Falls/PCT trails. (To reach Stuart Falls see #29 SEVEN-MILE TRAILHEAD TO STUART FALLS).

From the junction head southwest on McKie Camp Trail No. 1089 and gradually descend to McKie Meadow at 9.7 miles. There are some nice spots for camping near the meadow with a creek nearby. The creek flows year-round.

At 9.9 miles reach the junction of the McKie/Tom and Jerry trails. Continue on the McKie Camp Trail reaching the junction of McKie/Mudjekeewis trails another couple of hundred yards to the south. Keep left and head south on McKie Camp to Solace Meadow at 11.8 miles.

There is a campsite on the north end of the meadow and a year-round stream located nearby. Also, there is an old cabin near the junction of McKie Camp/Halifax trails. The cabin was built in the 1940's by local cattlemen and served as a line cabin for a grazing allotment. The cabin is approximately 12' by 16' and of pole and shake construction.

At this point the McKie Camp Trail heads southeast and back to PCT. To continue the loop follow Halifax Trail No. 1088 past the cabin and descend moderately through the trees. Continue descending via switchbacks which begin at 13.1 miles. Cross a creek at 14.4 miles then gradually descend to the Middle Fork Rogue River at 14.8 miles. Cross the river via two giant logs and continue up the trail where a sign, "Trail," points the way.

Hike up the steep hill to the Middle Fork Trail No. 978 at 14.9 miles. Turn left toward Alta Lake and follow the river as the trail gradually climbs. At 17.3 miles the trail curves away from the river and climbs moderately. The trail crosses many small streams into an area lush in ferns, flowers, deciduous trees and giant old-growth pines.

At 17.7 miles the switchbacks begin. During the next two miles the trail climbs moderately (sometimes steep) and switchback after switchback help to make this steep mountainside a bit easier to hike. The map shows a total of six switchbacks, but in reality you'll find there are about 28.

At 19.7 miles reach Alta Lake Trail No. 979. Turn left toward Alta Lake and gradually climb. At 20.2 miles reach the junction of King Spruce/Alta Lake trails. Continue a gradual climb past Boulder Pond at 21.0 miles. Reach Alta Lake at 21.6 miles. When you first reach Alta Lake walk over to the ridge to the east for a view into the Seven Lakes Basin and towards Crater Lake National Park.

Campsites are located at both ends of the lake which is over one-half mile long. Those wanting to cast in their fishing lines may catch a brook trout or two in this 32 acre lake.

To continue the loop, head south along the eastern shore of Alta Lake, reaching the south end of the lake at 22.2 miles. Reach the junction of Alta Lake/Seven Lakes Trail at 22.6 miles.

Descend moderately on the Seven Lakes Trail No. 981 to South Lake at 23.4 miles. A reforestation site is located on the southeast side of the lake so hikers are asked not to camp in this area. However, there is a "camping" sign located further down the trail which leads to a nice campsite.

Anglers, please note that five of the seven lakes in Seven Lakes Basin have been stocked with brook trout. North and South Lakes are the only lakes not currently stocked by the Oregon Dept. of Fish and Wildlife.

It's an easy hike to Cliff Lake and a magnificent view of Devils Peak at 23.7 miles. Again, there is a fine campsite on the west side of the lake with additional campsites on the south and east sides of the lake. Heavy reforestation has been implemented in some areas around the lake and camping is no longer permitted.

Continue past Cliff Lake to a junction at 23.9 miles. Turn left and descend slowly to the south end of Middle Lake at 24.2 miles. A trail loops around the south end of the lake and a sign asks that campers refrain from camping in the area due to "Boggy Lakeshores." Continue along the lake to the junction of Lake Ivern/Seven Lakes trails at 24.4 miles.

Continue straight on Seven Lakes Trail passing Grass Lake at 24.6 miles. There is a "Horse Camp" near here (a sign points the way) and a place to let horses graze farther down the trail. At 24.9 miles there is another "camping" sign leading to a site on the east side of Grass Lake.

Slowly climb to the junction of Seven Lakes/ PCT at 25.3 miles. Turn left onto the PCT and head towards Crater Lake. The trail is a series of gradual ups and downs, passing Honeymoon Creek at 25.9 miles. Continue to the PCT/Sevenmile Trail junction at 27.9 miles. Head northeast on the Sevenmile Trail descending to the trailhead at 29.7 miles.

Leafy-headed aster

31 SEVENMILE TRAILHEAD to SEVEN LAKES

Distance: 11.9 miles
Elevation gain: 1,500 feet; loss: 500 feet
High point: 6,600 feet
Usually open: Late June through October
Topographic map: Sky Lakes Wilderness
Obtain map from: Winema National Forest
Rogue River National Forest

Seven Lakes Basin is one of the most beautiful areas in the Sky Lakes Wilderness with deep blue lakes for fishing, swimming, and just plain taking-it-easy. And for those who like to be on top of things you'll find Devils Peak a short distance away. From atop Devils Peak, at 7,582 feet, you'll see all of Sky Lakes Wilderness and the mountains and valleys beyond. For those who crave solitude, please note that this area does get a lot of use, especially on holidays.

To reach the Sevenmile Trailhead travel 4 miles west on Nicholson Road from the small town of Fort Klamath, Oregon. Turn left on FS Road No. 3300 for 0.2 mile then turn right on FS Road No. 3334. Follow No. 3334 until it ends at the trailhead, 6 miles from Nicholson Road.

From the trailhead, hike Sevenmile Trail No. 3703 through the trees to the Wilderness boundary, 100 yards from the parking area. Continue the gradual climb to the junction of the Sevenmile/Pacific Crest Trail (PCT) at 1.8 miles.

Turn to the left and head southwest on the PCT, traveling the level trail to Honeymoon Creek at 3.8 miles. Continue the easy trail to the PCT/Seven Lakes Trail junction at 4.4 miles. Turn right on Seven Lakes Trail No. 981, continuing on to Grass Lake at 4.8 miles. Grass Lake is the first of the lakes we will see on this trail. At this point notice the "camping" sign leading to a nice campsite on the east side of the lake.

Backpackers please note that five of the seven lakes in Seven Lakes Basin have been stocked

with brook trout by the Oregon Department of Fish and Wildlife. North and South Lakes are the only two lakes not stocked with trout.

Continue further west along the trail reaching a "horse camp" sign at 5.1 miles. There is plenty of room for those packing in on horses and an area for grazing stock is located a short distance to the east of this point.

To continue to the remaining lakes, head west on the trail and reach the Lake Ivern/Seven Lakes trails at 5.3 miles. Middle Lake is located across the trail. Turn right on Lake Ivern Trail No. 994, cross a creek, and head up the trail to a "camping" sign at 5.5 miles. There are two fine sites here at the north end of Middle Lake. Both have a good view of the lake and Devils Peak looms in the background.

North Lake is located to the northwest of Middle Lake and can be reached by hiking via a side trail located on the north end of Middle Lake.

Back on trail, descend to another horse camp at 5.9 miles. The camp is to your left. A few hundred yards down the trail and you'll cross a creek with a sign reading "Horsefeed." There is a meadow to the right.

Continue descending to Jahn Spring at 6.5 miles where you may find summer wildflowers. Buckley Spring is located farther down the trail at 6.8 miles.

The trail is level as you reach the junction of Big Foot Spring at 7.0 miles. Big Foot Spring is located 0.2 mile down the trail at a moderate descent. Also, there are some fine spots for camping. Primitive furniture, probably made by hunters, litter some of the camp area. The Forest Service plans to tear these apart, but for the time being they are there.

Back on Lake Ivern Trail, continue a short descent to Lake Ivern at 7.2 miles. A trail winds around the east side of the lake providing access to a few campsites on the north side of the lake. Another campsite is located to the right and up the hill from the sign "camping." After you reach the campsite, a few hundred feet away, continue on the trail to Boston Bluff. The bluff is certainly large enough to camp on and the view is terrific, but the sharp rocks will probably prevent most people from camping here.

So far we've passed four of the seven lakes located in Seven Lakes Basin. To reach the remaining three, head back to the junction of Lake Ivern/Seven Lakes Trail at 9.1 miles.

The trail runs along the east side of Middle Lake and reaches the junction of the Cliff Lake Trail at 9.6 miles. Turn right, continuing on Seven Lakes Trail to Cliff Lake at 9.7 miles. When standing on the north shore of Cliff Lake

ll see Devils Peak in the background. This
on has been reforested so please use camp-
on the east, west, and south sides of the lake.
radually climb to South Lake at 10.1 miles
from there climb moderately to the junc-
of Seven Lakes / Alta Lake trails at 10.9
s. Turn right on Alta Lake Trail No. 979,
ng the level trail to Alta Lake at 11.3 miles.
ll reach the north end of this over half-mile
at 11.9 miles. There are campsites at both
of the lake and a particularly scenic view
the ridge located on the east side of the
h end of Alta Lake. From this point you can
he Seven Lakes Basin and beyond.

Fog from bluff near Alta Lake

32 NANNIE CREEK TRAILHEAD to PUCK LAKES

Distance: 2.6 miles
Elevation gain: 330 feet; loss: 0 feet
High point: 6,450 feet
Usually open: Late June through October
Topographic map: Sky Lakes Wilderness
Obtain map from: Winema National Forest
Rogue River National Forest

Golden mantled ground squirrel

There are two Puck Lakes to visit on this trip. Both North and South Puck Lakes are located at 6,450 feet in elevation and both are stocked with brook trout. South Puck Lake is the largest with 24 acres, but 7 acre North Puck Lake is the deepest of the two lakes with a depth of 18 feet.

To reach the Nannie Creek Trailhead travel north on Westside Road from Rocky Point, Oregon (located on the northwest shore of Upper Klamath Lake) to FS Road No. 3484. Turn left and follow Rd. 3484 until it ends at 5.5 miles.

The trail begins with a series of switchbacks for the first 0.8 mile then levels off. Reach South Puck Lake via forest-covered trail at 2.6 miles. North Puck Lake is located to the north of South Puck Lake. Level campsites can be found at both lakes.

33 TRAPPERS LAKE VIA THE CHERRY CREEK TRAIL

Distance: 5.0 miles
Elevation gain: 1,311 feet; loss: 0 feet
High point: 5,938 feet
Usually open: Late June through October
Topographic map: Sky Lakes Wilderness
Obtain map from: Winema National Forest
                 Rogue River National Forest

Trappers Lake is an excellent choice for fishing, swimming, and just plain relaxing. Luther Mountain rises to the west of Trappers Lake and appears to be but a stone's throw away. Yet looks can be deceiving, for between Trappers Lake and the mountain you'll find an unexpected surprise—Margurette Lake.

There are four trails leading into the Trappers Lake area with the Cherry Creek Trail leading directly to Trappers Lake from the east. The Cherry Creek Trail also provides the steepest route to the lake.

To reach the Cherry Creek Trailhead, take Westside Rd. north from Rocky Point (located on the northwest shore of Upper Klamath Lake) to FS Road No. 3450. Continue on FS Road No. 3450 until it ends at the trailhead at 2.0 miles.

Begin hiking along level Cherry Creek Trail No. 3708, reaching the Wilderness boundary at 0.7 mile. Cherry Creek, the creek for which this trail was named, flows along near the trail for the first 1.4 miles. Snow melt from Cherry Peak, the 6,623 foot mountain to the south of the trail, drains into the creek.

Follow the trail as it leads gradually through dense pine forest, small creeks (easy to ford) and open meadows. There are several larger streams and creeks to cross with bridges provided for easy access. Mosquitoes can be horrendous in this area so be sure to bring plenty of bug repellent.

At 3.5 miles the trail begins to climb at a rapid rate. After a 900 foot ascent the terrain levels off some and leads to the Sky Lakes Trail / Cherry Creek Trail junction at 5.0 miles. Trappers Lake is located just across the trail.

Your senses will go wild with your first peek at Trappers Lake. The rocky cliffs of Luther Mountain are reflected in the deep blue waters of this high mountain lake. Listen carefully and you'll hear the sound of birds chirping, squirrels calling, and maybe you'll see a deer browsing.

If you feel like swimming, take a dip. At 11 feet deep, Trappers Lake is just right for swimming. And if you have the urge for pan-fried trout, cast your line. The lake was recently stocked with brook trout.

While visiting Trappers Lake you may want to explore the surrounding area. Margurette Lake is only 0.2 mile from Trappers. Take Sky Lakes Trail No. 3762 around the north end of Trappers Lake and continue to the Divide Trail No. 3717. Margurette Lake is on your right.

Please obey the signs placed near the shore of Margurette Lake. Unwise campground practices have resulted in the depletion of some of the natural vegetation that once surrounded the lake. Efforts to revegetate this area and other areas with the same problem are in progress. Please help to make this effort successful.

If you're keen on spectacular views follow the Divide Trail No. 3717 to the south of Margurette Lake. Continue 0.2 mile to an unnamed lake on your right. Here the trail curves to the west for a short distance then heads north and begins to climb. The Divide Trail meets the Pacific Crest Trail (PCT) just 1.4 miles from Margurette Lake. The trail slopes upward 600 feet in elevation to a high of 6,600 feet at the PCT. Take advantage of the trail you're climbing and enjoy the splendid view of the surrounding countryside. (Please note, it is not necessary to hike all the way to the PCT to catch a view. The view is worth a trip after hiking just 0.5 mile from Margurette Lake.)

INTRODUCTION TO THE WILD ROGUE WILDERNESS

Cascading waterfalls, towering cliffs, rushing rapids, delicate wildflowers, abundant wildlife, and autumn colors all combine to make the Wild Rogue Wilderness a wonderful place to visit.

The Wild Rogue Wilderness is located in the southwest corner of Oregon with the southwest boundary of the Wilderness near the small town of Agness, Oregon, where those in need will find gas, food, fishing bait and tackle, and other essentials.

The 36,000 acre area was designated the Wild Rogue Wilderness on February 24, 1978, when Congress passed the Endangered American Wilderness Act. Two government agencies manage the Wilderness: the Siskiyou National Forest manages 26,500 acres, Bureau of Land Management 9,000 acres, and the remaining 500 acres are in private ownership.

There are two maintained trails found within the Wild Rogue Wilderness. The Panther Ridge Trail follows pine and rhododendron-covered Panther Ridge, located in the northern section of the Wilderness, and leads to Hanging Rock, a rock that has been likened to Yosemite's Half Dome. It's an easy climb to the top of Hanging Rock where you'll see endless valleys and mountains and the Wild Rogue Wilderness beyond. (See #35, PANTHER RIDGE TRAIL No. 1253 for details.)

The Rogue River Trail parallels the famous Rogue River which flows through the heart of the Wilderness. The 40-mile trail begins at Grave Creek and follows along the north bank of the river to Illahe. (See #34, THE ROGUE RIVER TRAIL NO. 1160, for directions on hiking the 15-mile section of trail located in the Wild Rogue Wilderness which stretches from Illahe to Marial.)

Those visiting the Wild Rogue Wilderness should note that this is unlike other Wilderness areas in that you'll find several lodges located along the river and motorboats are permitted on the Rogue River. For those hikers interested in spending a night or two at one of these rustic lodges, write to the Gold Beach Chamber of Commerce, listed at the end of this introduction.

The Rogue River was designated a Wild and Scenic River in 1978. At that time, however, Congress demanded that the River continue to be managed under the Wild and Scenic River act of 1968. You will see and hear motorboats downstream from Blossom Bar, but a hike up the river is still worthwhile.

The best time to hike the trail is in the spring or fall thus avoiding the hot summer months, as well as the many rafting parties that camp along the river. Permits are required for the 120 people launched into the river each summer day so crowds aren't as bad as they could be. The Forest Service maintains that "contacts are common, but conflicts are minimal."

Conflicts haven't always been minimal along the Rogue River. White men fought the Indians and the Indians lost. In 1859, gold was first discovered on the Rogue prompting prospectors to examine every inch along the river. Again, conflicts arose. Today, old mining relics, such as abandoned equipment, piles of stones along stream beds, and occasional shafts can be seen when you visit the Wilderness. And fur-trapping and homesteading combine with Indian wars and the lure of gold to make the Rogue's history a colorful one indeed.

The Rogue River is nationally-known for its tremendous fishing. The Rogue River serves as a liquid highway to salmon and steelhead, which migrate up the river to gravel beds appropriate for spawning. Young fish then journey to the ocean to grow to maturity, returning to the Rogue River so the cycle may be repeated once again.

Wildlife lovers will enjoy the black-tailed deer which feed in the Wilderness, sometimes coming right into camp. Black bear also live in the Wilderness and have been known to visit campsites. Incidents have occurred, so please use common sense and do not feed the wildlife. Other animals you might be lucky enough to observe include otter, Roosevelt elk, raccoon, squirrels, and other species.

An abundance of reptiles can be observed such as: lizards, skinks, newts, and salamanders, and on occasion you may see a ringneck snake, king snake, rattlesnake, or Pacific pond turtle.

Birders might see great blue herons fishing along the river's edge and common mergansers zooming by. Water ouzels, also known as dippers, may be seen scurrying from rock to rock or plunging underwater in search of food. In addition to these fine birds, you may also see bald eagles, ospreys, blue grouse, hummingbirds, and many others.

Wildflowers do their part during the spring and early summer months by decorating the Wilderness with their bright colors and unique shapes.

Poison oak is common along portions of the Rogue River Trail, but can be avoided and shouldn't be a problem to those who can identify the plant. Another annoyance to be aware of are wood ticks and mosquitoes. Wood ticks are numerous during the spring and summer months, and while there are mosquitoes, too, the Forest Service has not had any reports claiming that the mosquitoes are particularly bad at any time of year.

Horses are not allowed on the Rogue River Trail. The narrow trail and steep canyon walls makes travel by horse quite dangerous. If you want to visit the Wild Rogue River Wilderness by horseback please use the Panther Ridge Trail.

For an experience like no other try the Wild Rogue River Wilderness. For more information contact:

Siskiyou National Forest   or   Bureau of Land Management
1504 NW Sixth St.   310 West Sixth St.
P.O. Box 440   Medford, OR 97501
Grants Pass, OR 97426
(503) 479-5301

For lodging information write to:

Gold Beach Chamber of Commerce
510 South Ellensburg
Gold Beach, OR 97444

Rafting down the Rogue River near Blossom Bar

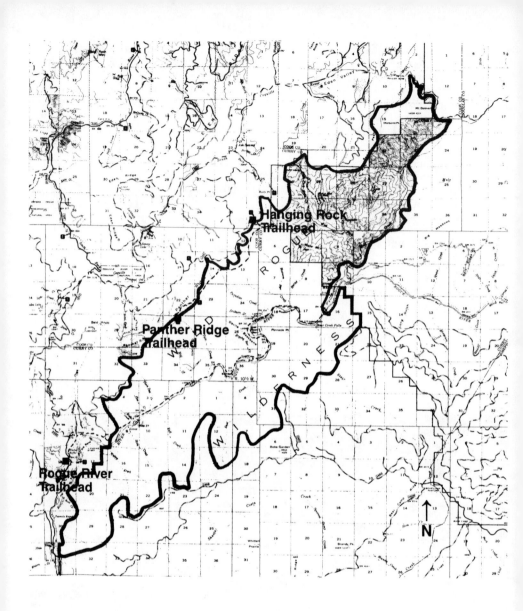

Hanging Rock
Trailhead

Panther Ridge
Trailhead

Rogue River
Trailhead

N

SOUTHERN OREGON WILDERNESS AREAS

34 ROGUE RIVER TRAIL NO. 1160

Distance: 15 miles
Elevation gain: 413 feet; **loss:** 188 feet
High point: 425 feet
Usually open: Year-round, but cold and rainy in winter, hot in the summer. Fall and spring are best.
Topographic map: Wild Rogue Wilderness Map
Obtain map from: Siskiyou National Forest

Sheer cliffs, white-water rapids, great fishing, bald eagles, deer, bear, and spectacular scenery combine to make the Rogue River Trail a backpacking experience that mustn't be missed.

To reach the Rogue River Trail take FS Road No. 33, to the bridge located three miles north of Agness, Oregon. Cross the bridge which takes you over the Rogue River and follow the right fork (County Road No. 375) towards Illahe. Pass the Illahe campground and the Foster Bar area before reaching the Rogue River Trailhead sign at 4.0 miles from the bridge.

The trailhead is clearly marked and a registration card is provided if you'd like to fill one out. Follow Rogue River Trail No. 1160 and reach a sign in 0.1 mile that says our destination—Marial—is just 15.0 miles away.

Cross the fence ladder near the sign and follow the trail as it passes through an apple orchard located on the old Billings Ranch. As you cross the field follow the U.S. Forest Service fencepost markers. Cross a fence ladder at 0.6 mile and shortly thereafter cross the bridge at Billings Creek.

Climb gradually and get a good view of the Rogue River at 1.4 miles. At 1.5 miles you'll cross Buster Creek and head through the trees, catch-

ing a glimpse of the Rogue now and then.

At 2.0 miles enter the Wilderness, although there isn't a sign there to tell you so. You'll also enter an area jam-packed with berry plants. Pick all you want when the berries ripen during midsummer.

The trail reaches Dans Creek in 2.4 miles. This is a nice, cool spot for lunch or a water break as the water is easy to get to. Just hike down to the creek before crossing the bridge.

The trail heads through the trees as you hike along the slope above the river. It's possible to view the river through the trees. At 2.8 miles you'll see the Wild River Lodge on the opposite side of the river. Head through the trees and at 3.1 miles you'll cross the bridge at Hicks Creek, another good source for water. And you'll have another great view of the river just before reaching Flea Creek at 3.8 miles.

Continue through the trees at 4.0 miles and you'll find a real treat at Flora Dell Creek. Here is a lovely little waterfall where you can forget about the hot summer sun and feel the cool breeze and cold mist.

The trail opens out onto a slope covered with trees which include the Oregon oak, the California black oak, and maple trees. The trees provide much needed shade in the summer and in the fall there are beautiful golds and reds for all to enjoy. There are also many views of the Rogue River along this portion of the trail as it heads across the semi-open slope.

You're back into the trees and crossing Almost Creek (sometimes dry) at 5.2 miles. The trail passes through the trees then back out onto the slope for a view of the river then back into the trees again. At 5.9 miles you'll see a few unfinished cabins and the Clay Hill Lodge. The trail crosses Clay Hill Creek then heads back out onto a long steep slope, sometimes covered with oaks, sometimes open.

Head back into the trees and reach Camp Tacoma at 6.5 miles. Just past the bridge crossing Camp Tacoma Creek you'll find two outhouses and a sign directing you to the camp. There are quite a few spots for camping at this site.

Continue through the trees to Tate Creek at 6.6 miles. There is a great little waterfall on this creek, visible if you climb down the embankment to river level. Continue on the trail through the trees then out onto an open area that follows the river around to Solitude Bar at 7.7 miles. Once there was an Indian village located at Solitude Bar; later the area was famous for early day mining. Swift water runs here making this a good spot to look for rafters and kayakers.

SOUTHERN OREGON WILDERNESS AREAS

You'll have a good view of the river just past Solitude Bar. Hike up the hill to a sign near the top that reads "Captain Tichnor's Defeat." This point was the site of a battle during the Rogue Indian War of 1855-56. Captain Tichnor led his party up the river to confront the Indians and was either soundly beaten or massacred states one report from the Forest Service. Another reports that the Indians were able to turn back Tichnor and his soldiers by using large rocks which they rolled down the mountain toward the white men.

At 8.6 miles the trail heads back into the trees to a moist, densely vegetated area. Cross Ivin Creek soon after entering the trees and continue to 8.9 miles and the Brushy Bar Creek. A trail heads 100 yards to the right. Here you'll find several nice campsites amid the dense greenery. Two outhouses are also provided. From this point it is only another 150 yards or so to the Rogue River. Back on the trail at 9.0 miles reach a sign pointing the way to the Brushy Bar Campground which consists of one nice secluded campsite and an outhouse nearby.

The trail continues in the trees past the Brushy Bar Guard Station than opens onto a steep slope with the Rogue River about 300 feet below. The trail remains on this high, open slope for over a mile then passes through the trees. At 11.4 miles the trail reaches an area almost level to the river. You might want to hike the short distance down to the river for a nice view and to cool off. Up the river a short ways is the Paradise Bar Lodge.

The trail heads through the trees to Jackson Creek at 11.7 miles. Cross here and at 11.8 miles reach the beginning of Paradise Bar. This is a wild turkey management area so please keep dogs on a leash. The trail continues along the back side of a ranch. At 12.2 miles cross a gate and at 12.3 miles cross the bridge at Paradise Creek.

Hike up the gradual slope through the trees to 12.8 miles. At this point the trail crosses another open slope above the Rogue River. Continue as the trail gradually descends then remains level. The trail heads back into the trees and just prior to 13.0 miles you'll see some good spots for camping on your right side. And for your convenience there is an outhouse on the left. Cross Blossom Bar Creek at 13.0 miles via the bridge. This is another good spot for water as the creek is easily accessible. Cross Burns Creek a few hundred yards down the trail.

The trail follows a shaded slope above the Rogue River for a mile then opens up to a treeless slope high above the Rogue River. At 14.2 miles you'll reach a breathtaking viewpoint at Inspira-tion Point. Looking due east, notice Stair Creek Falls located across the river. Continue for another 0.5 mile crossing mostly open slope and heading into the trees just prior to reaching the Mariel Trailhead at 15.0 miles.

Rogue River near Solitude Bar

35 PANTHER RIDGE TRAIL NO. 1253 (From Road No. 050 to Hanging Rock)

Distance: 5.5 miles
Elevation gain: 1,954 feet; loss: 1,200 feet
High point: 3,954 feet
Usually open: Year-round, but can be closed
from time to time by snow.
Call Powers Ranger District
for current conditions.
Topographic map: Wild Rogue Wilderness Map
Obtain map from: Siskiyou National Forest

The 10.8 mile Panther Ridge Trail is located in the northern portion of the Wild Rogue Wilderness. Approximately seventy-five percent of this trail is located within the Wilderness area, with the remaining sections of trail located on National Forest Land. The following guide will lead the hiker from a trailhead located 3.9 miles east of Bald Knob to the unique rock formation, Hanging Rock.

To reach the Panther Ridge Trailhead take FS Road No. 33, to the bridge located three miles north of Agness, Oregon. Cross the bridge which takes you over the Rogue River to the fork of FS Road No. 33 and County Road No. 375. Head to the left and up FS Road No. 33. Continue straight ahead when you reach Agness Pass at 2,354 feet. At 16 miles from the junction of Roads No. 33 and No. 375 you'll reach the junction of FS Road No. 3348 and FS Road No. 33. Turn right on FS Road No. 3348 (towards Eden Valley) and continue 2 miles to FS Road No. 5520. Turn right again and head to Panther Ridge Trailhead. After 2.6 miles turn right on FS Road No.

050. Stay on FS Road No. 050 to the "End of Road" sign. Turn right and park at the trailhead.

From the trailhead climb the dirt mound and head up the trail which looks like an old jeep trail. A sign points out Panther Ridge Trail No. 1253. Climb the steep, little used trail a short distance before reaching a junction and a better trail. The Bald Mountain L.O. is 3.8 miles to the west. Turn left to continue to Hanging Rock.

Continue on this easy trail through the trees and at 0.4 mile reach a dirt road. Follow this for a few hundred yards until the road forks. Take the dirt road to the right as you climb the moderate grade then level off. At 0.8 mile the trail heads through the trees then at 0.9 mile it crosses a dirt road and heads into the trees towards the northeast. There is a good view of the surrounding mountains off to the south just before crossing the road.

At 1.0 mile reach a Panther Ridge sign. Now the trail descends into an area rich in pines and rhododendrons. The trail winds up and down. At 2.0 miles you'll see a trail heading to the left. This trail leads to Panther Camp. A sign points the way to Panther Camp, but it is posted only for those heading from the opposite direction.

At 2.9 miles the trail climbs at a steep angle but luckily for only 0.1 mile. At 3.0 miles there is a good view of the valley to the south if you walk to the top of the ridge.

The trail descends a bit then continues through the trees. For the next couple of miles the trail climbs and descends at a moderate level. The vegetation is thick with rhododendrons and other plants. At 3.7 miles you'll get a view of Hanging Rock and the surrounding valley. Continue to 4.9 miles and the junction of Trail No. 1253A and Trail No. 1253. Trail No. 1253A leads to the Hanging Rock Trailhead, 0.3 mile away. Continue up Trail No. 1253 for a gradual climb to Hanging Rock Trail at 5.3 miles.

Follow the trail to Hanging Rock as it climbs and makes a long switchback at 5.5 miles. Those folks not afraid of heights will find Hanging Rock a cinch to climb. From the top, every hiker will be rewarded with a breathtaking view of the Wild Rogue Wilderness, Eden Valley and the forest beyond.

**Special Note: For those who'd rather not hike the 5.5 mile trail recommended here, there is an easier way to go. To reach the Hanging Rock Trailhead continue on Road No. 5520 for another 4.3 miles. Turn right on Road No. 5520/140 and continue to the Hanging Rock Trailhead just 1.4 miles ahead. Trail No. 1253A leads 0.3 mile to the jct. of Trail No. 1253 and No. 1253A which is discussed in the above text.

SOUTHERN OREGON WILDERNESS AREAS

Hiker on Hanging Rock

ACKNOWLEDGEMENTS

I received a great deal of assistance while preparing this book and I have many to thank. First of all, I want to thank the Lord. Leading me to accept and accomplish projects I never dreamed possible, Jesus holds my hand, steering me to walk the path He's laid before me.

Also, I'd like to thank the many Forest Service employees who answered my countless questions and provided much-needed literature on each Wilderness area. And a warm thanks must be given to Dee Westerberg from the Winema National Forest. The time she spent coordinating our trips into each Wilderness and her sincere interest in this project are greatly appreciated.

A special thanks must be given to my family and friends. To my parents, Beverly and Donald Ikenberry, and to my brothers, Don and Dave Ikenberry, thank you for your love, your support, for caring, for always being there for me, and for believing in me always. To my dearest and best friends, thank you for your love and friendship.

Also, I'd like to thank Stephanie Hakanson, Aspenwood Studios, for her wonderful service and skill in printing our black and white photographs for publication.

To Oral Bullard, my publisher, thank you for your help, guidance, and for always sending back a prompt reply. It's been a pleasure working with you.

And I must say thanks to my best pal, my Samoyed dog, Samuel. Not many dogs are asked to hike hundreds of miles in a few months time, but Sam hikes every mile I hiked, and never once complained.

And last, but certainly not least, I want to thank my husband, Roger. More than just a husband, he's my best friend and partner, and I thank him for the past 15 years and the many years to come.

Roger and Donna Aitkenhead with their Samoyed dog, Samuel